IT HAPPENED
FIRST IN VIRGINIA

IT HAPPENED
FIRST IN VIRGINIA

William O. Foss

Designed and Illustrated by
Janet Weiland Sturgill

THE
DONNING COMPANY
PUBLISHERS
NORFOLK/VIRGINIA BEACH

Books by William O. Foss:

It Happened First in Virginia
The United States Navy in Hampton Roads
The Norwegian Lady and the Wreck of the Dictator
Here is Your Hobby: Skiing

With co-authors:

Coast Guard in Action
Helicopters in Action
Marine Corps in Action
Skin Divers in Action
Oceanographers in Action

The Donning Company/Publishers
5659 Virginia Beach Boulevard
Norfolk, Virginia 23502

Designed and illustrated by
Janet Weiland Sturgill

Library of Congress Cataloging-in-Publication Data:

Foss, William O.   ata:
    It happened first in Virginia.

    Bibliography: p.
    Includes index.
    1. Virginia—History—Miscellanea. 2. World records.
I. Title.
F226.5.F67   1990   975.5   88-25823
ISBN 0 89865 674 5

Printed in the United States of America

To Dulcie, a Virginian

CONTENTS

ACKNOWLEDGMENTS

In researching material for this book, I literally looked high and low for information. Many Virginians responded to my queries and I am grateful for their generous assistance and suggestions.

I have consulted original sources as well as books, magazines, and newspapers. Much interesting material was found in such reputable publications as the *Virginia Magazine of History and Biography*, and the *Virginia Cavalcade*.

I am indebted to the many leads offered by the doyen of first facts, Joseph Nathan Kane, in his superior collection, *Famous First Facts*, published by the H. Wilson Company, New York.

Other "first" leads were found in *Virginia Oddities* by T. Beverly Campbell, published by the Dietz Printing Co., Richmond.

Also useful was *Virginia First* by Dr. Lyon G. Tyler, published by the Colonial Dames of America in the State of Virginia.

Another book, *Virginia Leads*, published by the Virginia Division, United Daughters of the Confederacy, contains a multitude of first facts about the Commonwealth of Virginia.

W. O. F.

PREFACE

History is the memory of the past—the recording of great, near great, and not so great events. While we may not be serious about our reading of history, the public generally shows a curious interest in "first" historical events. Our fascination with people being first assures those who achieve something first, whether it is something noble or something despicable, that their deeds will be duly recorded for posterity.

Virginia and Virginians have racked up an impressive record of firsts, which continue to grow as new histories are written. Serendipity can be credited for some first events which took place in Virginia, because, as William Byrd once wrote, "in the beginning, all America was Virginia." But as you shall see in the stories herein, first events in Virginia were more often caused by strong and persuasive people whose deeds shaped events, rather than by people who followed the crowd.

The seed for this book was planted when I researched a book on the naval history of Hampton Roads. I found that Virginia led the nation in naval developments. Further research revealed that a significant number of first events in American history took place in Virginia. This book presents a variety of Virginia firsts, some of historical importance, others of a curiosity nature.

W. O. F.

AGRICULTURE

FIRST COMMERCIAL CULTIVATION OF TOBACCO

America's commercial involvement with tobacco began in the Virginia colony when John Rolfe grew his first experimental crop of tobacco in Jamestown in 1612.

Rolfe, celebrated as the husband of Indian princess Pocahontas, was a pipe smoker who had probably acquired the habit in England where tobacco had been introduced from Spanish-held territories in the New World. Rolfe arrived in Jamestown in May 1610.

While British pipesmokers enjoyed their Spanish tobacco, their king, James I, who did not like tobacco, in 1604 wrote a pamphlet against "this base and vile use of taking tobacco in our kingdom." King James wrote that smoking was "a custome Lothsome to the eye, hatefull to the Nose, harmful to the braine, daungerous to the Lungs, and in the black, stinking fume thereof, nearest resembling the horrible Stigian smoke of the pit that is bottomelesse."

The royal blast was of no concern to Rolfe, who decided to grow the tobacco that the Indians were already growing in the Virginia colony. Rolfe's first tobacco crop may have been for his own use. The colonists described that leaf, a strong tobacco now known as *Nicotiana rustica*, as "poore and weake, and of a byting tast." It could not compete in England and Europe with the milder Spanish leaf.

Sometime in 1612 John Rolfe acquired tobacco seeds from Spanish colonies in Trinidad and Venezuela. Of tobacco that grew from those seeds, Rolfe developed a desirable large-leaf plant, which was said to be as "strong, sweet and pleasant as any under the sun."

First shipments from Rolfe's experimental crop of mild *Nicotiana tabacum* reached England in 1613. Although only a few hundred pounds, it excited London merchants immediately. The merchants offered to buy as much tobacco as Jamestown could produce, so settlers threw their energies into growing leaf to the exclusion of all else. The fortified areas within the palisades were crowded with tobacco plants, while even the streets of Jamestown were utilized by the eager planters.

In 1615, some twenty-three hundred pounds of tobacco were shipped out from Jamestown, and in 1617 the *George* set sail for England laden with twenty thousand pounds of Virginia leaf.

England, which had been buying her tobacco from Spain, now decided that the colonial tobacco would be of economical benefit to the nation. Not only would her own people be supplied with colonial tobacco, but her merchant marine would be enriched by exporting tobacco to foreign countries. Thus tobacco, first cultivated by John Rolfe, became the most important commodity of the Virginia colony.

Today, as in colonial times, the golden leaf is a commodity of great economic, social, and fiscal importance to Virginia. The Old Dominion today grows four types of tobacco: flue-cured, used mainly in domestic blended cigarettes; burley, also a part of the American blended cigarette; fire-cured, used in snuff and chewing tobacco; and sun-cured, also used for chewing tobacco.

FIRST PRACTICAL MECHANICAL REAPER

A peaceful revolution that spread benefits to all corners of the earth had its start in Virginia's Shenandoah Valley on July 25, 1831. That's when Cyrus Hall McCormick demonstrated the world's first successful mechanical reaper on a crop of oats on the farm owned by John Steele of Steele's Tavern near Walnut Grove.

Others, including Cyrus McMormick's father, Robert McCormick, had tried to develop a reaping machine. Cyrus's machine was the first reaper that included all the basic parts of the modern grain-cutters: the straight reciprocating knife, guards, reel, platform, main wheel, side-moving cutter, and divider at the outer end of the cutter bar.

The elder McMormick had first begun his experiments while Cyrus was still a small boy. He first developed a pusher-type reaper in 1816; later he designed a thresher and other mechanical farm devices. As Cyrus grew up, he began to help his father with these projects.

Working in a blacksmith shop, Cyrus tinkered with various

Here is the birthplace of Cyrus Hall McCormick, near Steele's Tavern in the Shenandoah Valley. In the stone and log blacksmith shop seen here, along with the restored grist mill, McCormick in 1831, built the world's first successful horse-drawn mechanical reaper. Courtesy of the Virginia Division of Tourism

mechanical devices. By the time he was twenty-two years old he had designed an improved hillside plow, and built and demonstrated the first practical reaper.

Up to the time when Cyrus McCormick revealed his new invention, grain had been harvested by farmers using their scythes and sickles. Harvesting was hard work and required many days and weeks before the job could be finished. When McCormick demonstrated his horse-drawn reaper on John Steele's farm, he cut six acres of oats in one day.

While McCormick considered the first test of his reaper "a very successful experiment," he was not satisfied with his machine. He continued to make improvements and more tests before he applied for a patent, which the United States granted him on June 21, 1834.

Another inventor, Obed Hussey, had designed a reaper some time before McCormick received his patent, and the two engaged in severe competition, which McCormick won because he produced a superior harvesting machine.

At first McCormick constructed his reapers at Walnut Grove, but in 1843 he began issuing licenses to individuals in different parts of the country to manufacture the machines. This proved to be a mistake, because he was unable to control the quality of the reapers, and poorly constructed machines were giving his invention a bad name.

In 1847, Cyrus McCormick decided to move his production of reapers from Virginia to Chicago in order to be nearer the country's largest farm equipment market—the wide prairie grain fields.

He erected his own reaper factory in Chicago, and by 1850 had virtually cornered the national market for grain harvesting machines. By 1902, McCormick's company became International Harvester.

McCormick was one of the great pioneers in modern business management. He not only provided farmers with a labor-saving harvesting machine, but also introduced new marketing techniques—easy credit so farmers could pay for machines from increased crops, written performance guarantees, and advertising to convince skeptical farmers.

Cyrus McCormick's mechanical reaper and his new business methods helped make American farmers the most efficient in the world.

ARTS/ENTERTAINMENT

FIRST THEATRICAL PRODUCTION

Show business got off to a slow start in America. In the early days of the Virginia colony, play-acting was considered repugnant to good morals. In a prayer offered by the Anglican church on behalf of the infant colony in 1612, actors were referred to as belonging to the "scum and dregs of the earth."

With the restoration of the Stuart dynasty to the throne in England, the theater was again becoming a popular institution in both England and America.

While there apparently were appearances of amateur plays and strolling players in the Virginia colony, the first record of a theatrical performance was noted in the court records of Accomack County in 1665.

An aspiring playwright, William Darby, authored a play he called, *Ye Bare and ye Cubb*, then together with Cornelius Wilkinson and Philip Howard, performed the play on a Sunday afternoon, August 27, 1665, in Cole's Tavern in the town of Pungoteague.

Unfortunately, there exists no copy of the play, but three months later, Edward Martin, a pious Quaker, complained that the play was an "immoral" act to the King's attorney, John Fawsett, who ordered the three men arrested by the high sheriff. Bail was set for Wilkinson and Howard, but Darby was remanded to jail to await the hearing.

The men were ordered to appear in court on January 16, 1666, wearing those "habilements that they then acted in and give a draught of such verses or speeches which were then acted by them."

After the three players gave the judges a dress performance, the justices found the play harmless, and the actors were adjudged "not guilty of fault" and acquitted.

The justices were not pleased with Edward Martin for the trouble he had caused. They ordered him to pay all the costs incurred, including those for keeping playwright Darby in jail while awaiting trial.

FIRST PLAYHOUSE IN AMERICA

In 1716, the first playhouse in America was erected in Williamsburg. The theater was built by William Levingston near the Governor's Palace.

Impresario Levingston entered into a contract with Charles and Mary Stagg, dancing teachers, to produce "comedies, drolls, and other kind of stage plays...as shall be thought fitt to be acted there."

Plays were performed chiefly during the gay social seasons that accompanied the sessions of the General Court and the General Assembly, when visitors doubled the population of Williamsburg.

Though Levingston's theater was used for both professional and amateur productions, it was frequently in financial difficulties. Levingston was forced to mortgage the property in 1721 and to give up the theater and leave Williamsburg in 1727.

The building continued to be used periodically, but in 1745 it was presented to the city to be used as a town hall. The building was razed in 1770.

FIRST STATE THEATRE

The Barter Theatre in Abingdon, a small historic town situated in the mountains of Southwest Virginia, is one of the most unique and adventurous repertory theatres in America. It is America's longest-running professional resident theatre and the first state theatre in the nation.

The Barter Theatre got its start during the Great Depression in 1933 when an out-of-work, but enterprising young actor named Robert Porterfield reasoned that he and his fellow actors shouldn't go hungry in New York when there was an abundance of food in his native Virginia.

Porterfield, whose home was in nearby Saltville, envisioned that local farmers, who were unable to get cash for their crop, would be willing to trade their farm products for an evening of entertainment by professional (and starving) actors.

In this photograph, taken circa 1937, the audience barters their produce and livestock for tickets to see a play at the Barter Theatre in Abingdon. The Barter Theatre staged its first performance on June 30, 1933. Courtesy of the Barter Theatre

So, during the grim summer of 1933, Porterfield left New York and returned to his family home, bringing with him twenty-two fellow actors and a dream. The actors carried with them some scenery obtained from a cancelled road company. In Abingdon, Porterfield obtained the use of an old building, which was first constructed as a church from 1831 to 1833. After the congregation moved out, the building was later used as a temperance hall and a city hall, and had been known as the Opera House.

After readying the building for its first theatre production, Porterfield and his actors went around the town and tacked up posters advertising admission for thirty-five cents or the equivalent in produce: "With vegetables you cannot sell, you can buy a good laugh."

On June 30, 1933, the Barter Theatre opened its doors with John Golden's play, *After Tomorrow*, to a full house of farmers, mountaineers, and a few tourists. Taking Porterfield up on his offer of swapping produce for theatre tickets, the first-nighters paid their way with country hams, baskets of eggs, honey, fruits, homemade pickles and jams, a devil's food cake, a rooster, and a squealing pig. Legend has it that the sow pig became Barter Theatre's mascot and whose descendants provided royalties for several seasons of Barter productions.

The Barter players toured area towns during the week and returned to Abingdon's former town hall on weekends. The practice of trading "ham for *Hamlet*" caught on quickly. By the end of their first season, the Barter had cleared $4.35 in cash, two barrels of jelly, and a collective weight gain of over three hundred pounds.

As years passed, Abingdon's Barter Theatre thrived, gaining a solid reputation for quality. Comedies and dramas, classics and musicals were presented by professional actors, learning and creating in the highlands of Virginia. As Barter's reputation grew, the theatre became known as a training ground for countless hopefuls, many of them destined for fame. Among them are Gregory Peck, Patricia Neal, Ernest Borgnine, Fritz Weaver, Elizabeth Wilson, and Ned Beatty. Playwrights, in lieu of royalty fees, often accepted barter in the form of a Virginia ham as payment. One exception was George Bernard Shaw, a vegetarian who was sent a crate of spinach.

As the Depression waned, box office receipts became less edible and easier for accountants to add. In the early 1940s, Porterfield began promoting the cultural merits of the Barter Theatre to the Virginia Assembly, and in 1946 the State Legislature voted the Barter Theatre an appropriation of ten thousand dollars. The act designated the

Barter Theatre as the *"State Theatre of Virginia,"* the first in the nation.

Since then, Barter has received some government support, currently through the Virginia Commission for the Arts and the National Endowment for the Arts. A not-for-profit organization, Barter also receives funds from corporate grants and private contributions.

Today, as they did in 1933, Abingdon area natives and visitors continue to enjoy live theatre presented by top professional actors from the worlds of Broadway, film, and television. And although cash is the accepted exchange for a ticket at the box office, one can still barter one's way into the theatre with a ham, a bushel of potatoes, or a jar of preserves.

When the Barter Theatre in Abingdon received state support in 1946 it was designated "The State Theatre of Virginia," the first state theatre in the nation. Courtesy of the Barter Theatre

FIRST STATE-SUPPORTED ART MUSEUM

In 1786, a French scholar, Chevalier Alexandre-Marie Quesnay de Beaurepaire, established in Richmond the Academy of Arts and Sciences of America, with a charter from King Louis XVI. It was built at a site bounded by Broad, Twelfth, and Marshall streets.

Quesnay was one of the first French emigrants to Richmond to volunteer in 1776 for service in the American Revolution.

The academy, which was the first of its kind in America, offered courses in architecture, astronomy, chemistry, medicine, natural history, mineralogy, foreign languages, painting, and sculpture.

While the academy failed after one year of operation, it planted the seeds for a greater appreciation of art and culture in Virginia, leading eventually to the establishment of the nation's first state-supported art museum, the Virginia Museum of Fine Arts.

The concept for the Virginia Museum emerged in 1919, when Judge John Barton Payne gave his multi-million dollar collection of fifty paintings to the Commonwealth. Judge Payne, a native of what is now West Virginia, grew up in Fauquier County, had held several positions, including the Under Secretary of the Interior, in the Wilson Administration. He had also been chairman of the American Red Cross.

Gifts from others followed, and thirteen years later Judge Payne proposed a $100,000 challenge grant aimed at financing construction of a museum for Virginia's fledgling art collection.

The challenge was accepted by Gov. John Garland Pollard, who led a campaign to solicit the additional funds from private individuals, and who fought for state appropriations to subsidize the new museum's operating expenses. With these funds, as well as a grant from the Federal Works Project Administration, Judge Payne's dream became a reality, and on January 16, 1936, the first director, Thomas C. Colt, Jr., opened the doors of the museum's new Georgian building to the public for the first time.

Since its establishment, the Virginia Museum of Fine Arts has achieved a nationwide reputation for creative and innovative arts programming. The Museum's list of innovations is a lengthy and impressive one. The first performing arts facility inside a fine arts complex was built in the museum in 1954. The institution was an early trend-setter in creating orientation theatres in its permanent galleries and was the first museum in the country to develop "artmobiles" as tools to extend its collection and programs beyond the walls of the museum.

Through its acquisition program, which relies solely on private contributions, the Virginia Museum of Fine Arts has assembled a rich and varied permanent collection that provides a panoramic view of world art.

The Virginia Museum of Fine Arts as it looked when it first opened its doors to the public on January 16, 1936. The Museum is the nation's first state-supported art museum. It is located at Boulevard and Grove Avenue in Richmond. Courtesy of the Virginia Museum of Fine Arts

This depicts the Boulevard entrance foyer of the Virginia Museum of Fine Arts in 1936. The Museum has direct lineage from the Academy of Arts and Sciences of America, established in Richmond in 1786 by a French scholar. Courtesy of the Virginia Museum of Fine Arts

Judge John Barton Payne is the patron saint of the Virginia Museum of Fine Arts. In 1919, Judge Payne donated his collection of fifty paintings to the Commonwealth; in 1932 he offered a $100,000 challenge grant to build the Museum. Courtesy of the Virginia Museum of Fine Arts

Thomas C. Colt, Jr., (back row, sixth from left), the first director of the Virginia Museum of Fine Arts, is shown with members of his staff at the Boulevard entrance to the Museum. Courtesy of the Virginia Museum of Fine Arts

FIRST TRAVELING ARTMOBILE

The first exhibition of the nation's first Artmobile, organized and operated by the Virginia Museum of Fine Arts in Richmond, opened for public showing in Fredericksburg on October 13, 1953. The exhibition, "Little Dutch Masters," featured works by sixteenth and seventeenth-century Dutch and Flemish painters. Gov. John S. Battle participated in the opening ceremonies.

Wanting to bring art to regional centers which otherwise would have no opportunity to see original works of high caliber, the Virginia Museum borrowed a leaf from the bookmobile, and designed a self-contained art trailer which would be able to visit every community throughout the state.

The forty-five foot tractor trailer unit was donated to the Virginia Museum by the Miller & Rhoads department store, while the Virginia Federation of Women's Clubs made financial contributions toward meeting the initial operating costs.

By 1955, the first artmobile had taken the exhibition of Dutch and Flemish painters to fifty-five locations throughout the state. Today the museum operates three artmobiles, which have proven particularly successful in smaller communities which are far removed from major art resources. They are used extensively by the schools, and they are often at fairs and festivals.

Children view dutch
and Flemish paintings
exhibited by the first
Artmobile. Children are
often deeply impressed
by their first-hand con-
tact with the fine arts.
Courtesy of the Virginia
Museum of Fine Arts

This is the exterior view
of the nation's first
Artmobile operated by
the Virginia Museum of
Fine Arts. The Artmo-
bile opened its first exhibition at Fredericksburg
on October 13, 1953.
Courtesy of the Virginia
Museum of Fine Arts

The rambling wood-frame eighteenth century Hanover Tavern today houses the Barksdale Theatre, the nation's first dinner theatre. The original tavern was built in 1723 as an inn and stagecoach stop. Patrons of the inn included Jefferson, Lafayette, Washington, and Lord Cornwalis. Patrick Henry married the daughter of the proprietor, John Shelton, and lived here three years. The tavern was renovated in 1953 as a professional theatre and the first production was in 1954. Courtesy of the Virginia Division of Tourism

FIRST DINNER THEATRE

The Barksdale Theatre, the nation's first dinner theatre, was founded November 18, 1953, when six Wayne State University actor alumni purchased the Hanover Tavern in Hanover.

The colonial tavern, built in 1723, was first owned by William Parks of Williamsburg, printer-founder of the Virginia *Gazette*, and John Shelton, father-in-law of Patrick Henry.

The young actors purchased the Hanover Tavern as a site for their playhouse named for Barbara Barksdale of Charlottesville, a classmate who died of multiple sclerosis.

While the actors went about repairing the derelict tavern, they staged productions for private groups. It wasn't until September 16, 1954, that *Gold in the Hills*, their first public play, was presented. The play was presented on the first floor of the ball room, with the audience seated at small tables, to simulate a beer garden.

Two years later, in 1956, the Barksdale Theatre began serving food and thus became the first dinner theatre in the country.

Unlike the policies of many dinner theatres that followed the Barksdale, patrons at the Hanover Tavern did not have to purchase the entire dinner-and-theatre package. The play was the important part, but the food was delicious, and all menus were based on old tried-and-true Virginia recipes.

FIRST ALL-COUNTRY MUSIC RADIO STATION

Radio station WCMS began broadcasting from Norfolk on July 1, 1954, as the nation's first radio station to play nothing but country music. The very first record ever played on WCMS airwaves was Bill Monroe's "Blue Moon of Kentucky." The record was spun by disc jockey Teddy Crutchfield.

WCMS, first licensed to broadcast from sunrise to sunset at 1050 AM, was owned and operated by Cy Blumenthal and his partners, Ray Armand Kovitz, George A. Crump, and Connie B. Gay. Their plan to play continuously programmed country music was met with much skepticism, but their pioneering effort caught the public's fancy, and dubious advertisers eventually came around to buying air time.

WCMS helped to generate record sales and developed and sponsored live concerts by upcoming and established country music entertainers. By 1962, the station could bill itself as "America's Number One Country Music Station."

FM transmissions were added in 1964. The station played its one millionth record, "Where Does the Good Time Go" by Buck Owens, on January 31, 1967.

The first five disc jockeys of WCMS, the nation's first radio station to play nothing but country music, line up to be photographed for their 1954 Christmas greet- ings card. The young man in the middle, Teddy Crutchfield, spun the first record ever played on WCMS air- waves on July 1, 1954. Other WCMS disc jockeys are, from left to right Sheriff Tex Davis, Ted Harding, Art Barrett, and Ted Tater. Courtesy of WCMS

FIRST STALACPIPE ORGAN

The Great Stalacpipe Organ deep in the heart of Luray Caverns is the world's first and largest musical instrument using stalactite formations, which hang from cave ceilings, for tone sources in the instrument.

(Stalactites are rocky formations shaped like icicles by drippings of calcium carbonate. Stalagmite is a deposit of calcium carbonate like an inverted stalactite. These ageless rock formations in the Luray Caverns have been shaped at the rate of one cubic inch each 120 years.)

The idea of getting music from these rock formations evolved years ago when Leland W. Sprinkle, an electronic scientist and accomplished organist, took his son for a tour of the Luray Caverns. After hearing the clear, mystic tone when his guide tapped a stalactite, Sprinkle envisioned a musical instrument that would release the music of these majestic formations for all the world to hear.

Sprinkle told officials of the Caverns of Luray that he could create an instrument which would get its tone from the stalactites themselves. While skeptical at first, the officials agreed to let him try.

Selecting one of the larger sections of the caverns, Sprinkle discovered that only two of the stalactites were naturally in tune.

Sprinkle had to figure out a way of tuning the others. A system of grinding was worked out, with aluminum oxide sanding disks rotated at high speed.

Then, using a set of thirteen English tuning forks, Sprinkle tested and skillfully ground the different shaped stalactites in the sixty-four acre caverns until they would be in perfect pitch to produce stereophonic music.

From tuning of the stalactites, Sprinkle went on to develop the various octave chassis for his Great Stalacpipe Organ. The driving chassis for each octave is a complete and separate block, with power supply, electron tubes, and firing apparatus.

The tuned stalactite formation produce tones of symphonic quality and accuracy when tapped by rubber-tipped plungers under the organist's control. The Great Stalacpipe Organ can be played from a large organ console or by automatic control which faithfully carries out the interpretation of the organist.

"A Mighty Fortress Is Our God" was the first musical composition played on the Great Stalacpipe Organ on July 14, 1956.

Many weddings have been conducted in the Caverns to the music of this unique instrument.

The Luray Caverns were discovered on August 13, 1878, by an exploring party led by Andrew Campbell and Benton Stebbins of Luray.

The Great Stalacpipe Organ in the Luray Caverns is the world's only musical instrument which utilizes stalactites for tone sources in the instrument. A musical composition was first played on this underground organ on July 14, 1956. Courtesy of Luray Caverns Corporation

FIRST NATIONAL PARK FOR THE PERFORMING ARTS

The nation's first and only national park for the performing arts, the Wolf Trap Farm Park for the Performing Arts, in Vienna, near Washington, D.C., opened July 1, 1971, with a gala performance at the Filene Center, its outdoor theater. Since then, the park has gained worldwide recognition for its success in providing the finest in the performing arts in a beautiful setting.

In 1968, Mrs. Catherine Filene Shouse, who had bought the Wolf Trap Farm property in 1930, donated to the U.S. Government one hundred acres of her farmland, including buildings on the land, and funds for construction of the Filene Center. Her gift was accepted by an act of Congress in 1966. In 1981, Mrs. Shouse also donated additional land and funds for The Barns (two rustic New England barns) to make Wolf Trap a year-round center for the performing arts and related educational programs.

Mrs. Shouse, who was born in Boston in 1896, credits her parents, Mr. and Mrs. Lincoln Filene, for her interest in civic and cultural affairs. Her father was one of the original owners of Boston's famous Filene's department store.

The National Symphony Orchestra, with Julius Rudel conducting, performed at the opening of the Filene Center on July 1, 1971. Van Cliburn was the pianist, Norman Triegle was the bass-baritone. Other performers at the grand opening of the Wolf Trap Farm Park for the Performing Arts were the Washington Choral Arts Society, the Madison Madrigal Singers, and the U.S. Marine Band and Color Guard.

Filene Center, which quickly gained international recognition as a showcase for presenting a wide variety of the performing arts at affordable prices, burned to the ground in April 1982. The rebuilt and improved Filene Center reopened in July 1984. The new open pavilion seats thirty-eight hundred people under cover and three thousand on the lawn, where patrons can picnic while watching a performance.

Outside of the Filene Center, woodland trails lead visitors down to Wolf Trap Creek and the pond. There is the Children's Theatre-in-the-Woods and the Concert Shell in the meadow which host free programs for children during the summer.

For adults, free previews before many of the Filene Center shows give patrons an opportunity to hear lectures about the performance thereby gaining insight into the arts.

Open during the fall, winter, and spring months, The Barns of

Wolf Trap hosts a variety of programs from folk to classical, as well as monthly square dances.

As a national park, Wolf Trap falls under the jurisdiction of the Department of the Interior and is maintained by the National Park Service. The Wolf Trap Foundation, a non-profit organization created by Congress in 1968, is responsible for administration and programming needs for the park.

Mrs. Catherine Filene Shouse donated land and funds to establish America's first and only national park for the performing arts, the Wolf Trap Farm Park for the Performing Arts in Vienna, near Washington, D.C.
Courtesy of the Wolf Trap Foundation

Filene Center, amphitheatre at the Wolf Trap Farm Park for the Performing Arts, the nation's first and only national park for the performing arts, presented its first public performance on July 1, 1971. Burned in 1982, it was rebuilt and reopened in 1984. Courtesy of the Wolf Trap Foundation

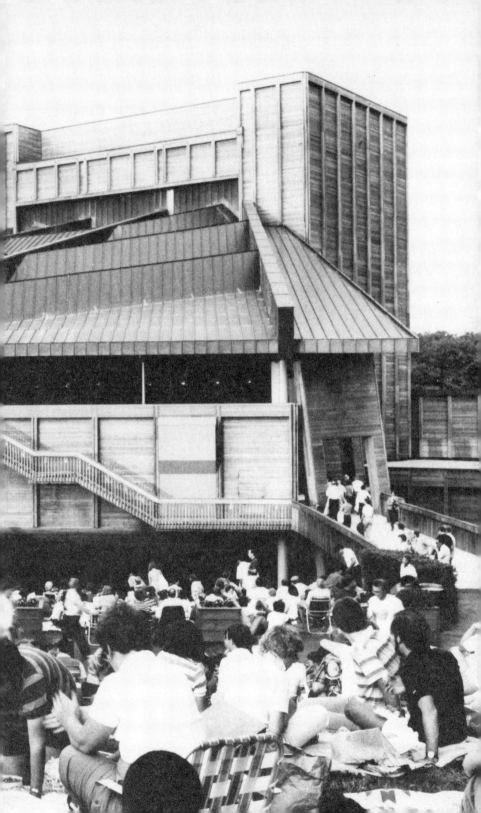

AVIATION

FIRST SUSTAINED FLIGHT OF A
HEAVIER-THAN-AIR MACHINE

An important but almost forgotten event in the development of the airplane took place May 6, 1896, on the Potomac river just off Quantico.

It was the first sustained flight in history of a heavier-than-air machine.

The machine was not a man-carrying aircraft, but an unmanned model resembling a giant dragonfly. The importance of this first flight was that it proved that flight by a heavier-than-air craft was possible.

The feat was accomplished by Samuel Piermont Langley, a renowned astronomer and secretary of the Smithsonian Institution, whose research of aerodynamics (a word he coined) had convinced him that it was possible to build a machine that would fly.

During his early aerodynamics experiments, Langley built rubberband-powered models sporting various wings, tail, and propeller combinations.

Langley even constructed a larger steam-powered "aerodrome," as he called it. In 1893, he decided to launch Model Number 4, a steam-powered aerodrome, into the wind from a fishing scow he had constructed on the Potomac River off Quantico. Several attempts with a spring-mounted launching apparatus failed.

Undaunted, Langley deduced that the aerodrome should have two sets of wings, each of equal area. On May 6, 1896, Aerodrome Model Number 5 was placed on the fishing scow while Langley, his mechanics and some close friends, including telephone inventor Alexander Graham Bell, watched.

Using a catapult device, Aerodrome Model Number 5 propelled

down the track and slowly rose into the wind over the Potomac River. Rising to a height of one hundred feet it flew a little over half a mile in about one and one-half minutes. The flight ended only because the gasoline used to generate steam to drive the propellers ran out. Nevertheless, Langley had achieved the first sustained flight in history of a heavier-than-air machine.

In 1898, at the request of the War Department, Langley began work on a man-carrying airplane. He first experimented with a one-quarter scale model and a smaller engine, and one of his models flew successfully in 1901.

However, when he built a man-carrying aircraft, it twice failed to fly. His last attempt to launch a man-carrying aircraft failed on December 8, 1903. Using an 850 pound aircraft and a catapult track eighty-five feet long, and friend Charles Manley, as pilot, Langley's aircraft just barely cleared the track before it plunged into the icy Potomac River.

Nine days later, on December 17, Orville and Wilbur Wright succeeded where Langley failed—they made the first manned flight in a heavier-than-air machine at Kitty Hawk, North Carolina.

Langley's pioneering work in aviation did not go unheeded. After Langley's death in 1906, Wilbur Wright wrote that "the fact that the great scientist, Professor Langley, believed in flying machines was the one thing that encouraged us to begin our studies."

A grateful nation has honored Samuel Piermont Langley in various ways. The Aviation Experimental Station and Proving Ground in Hampton became Langley Field in 1917. In 1922, the U.S. Navy named its first aircraft carrier the USS *Langley*. In 1947, the international unit of radiant energy was called the "Langley."

The National Aeronautical Space Administration (NASA) at Langley Air Force Base is called the Langley Research Center.

FIRST DIRIGIBLE PURCHASED BY THE U.S. GOVERNMENT

The first dirigible to be purchased by the U.S. government was first demonstrated at Fort Myer in Arlington on August 12, 1908, before representatives of the War Department.

Piloting the airship was Thomas Scott Baldwin, one of America's earliest dirigible enthusiasts. The engineer was Glenn H. Curtiss, who had built the dirigible's engine.

The dirigible constructed by Baldwin was designated the SC-1. It was subsequently purchased by the War Department for use by the

Signal Corps, which operated the airship at Omaha, Nebraska, for several years.

The envelope of the ninety-six-foot long dirigible was covered with a fabric made of silk and rubber. It contained twenty thousand cubic feet of hydrogen gas. The dirigible had a total lift of 1,360 pounds.

Baldwin and Curtiss flew the airship around the Fort Myer area for two hours at a speed of sixteen miles per hour.

Curtiss never became enamored of the prospects for dirigibles. He considered the airships fun, but "too slow for me." Curtiss, who was then well known for racing motorcycles and building engines, would soon become one of the nation's top aircraft manufacturers.

FIRST AIRPLANE FATALITY

In early 1908, Orville and Wilbur Wright, inventors of the first successful airplane, signed a contract with the War Department to provide aircraft for the U.S. Army. During September 1908, Orville Wright conducted a series of test flights with his Flyer biplane for the Army at Fort Myer in Arlington.

To the crowd of military officials and public spectators, Orville successfully demonstrated his new two-seater aircraft in brilliant flights over the Fort Myer parade ground.

On September 17, 1908, the last day of the flight demonstrations at Fort Myer, Orville Wright made several flights in which he carried a passenger. The Army wanted to see how the airplane could be used as an observation platform.

One of the passengers in the observation seat was Army lieutenant Thomas Selfridge, a twenty-six year-old aviation enthusiast who had worked with aircraft pioneer Glenn Curtiss and inventor Alexander Graham Bell in the Aerial Experiment Association.

After takeoff, Orville Wright and Selfridge circled the Fort Myer ground three times at an altitude of 125 feet. As they made the last turn toward the parade ground, the propeller cracked, leading to a chain reaction of mechanical failures. Wright cut the engine and although he tried to control the airplane, it smashed into the ground, breaking up as it ploughed forward in a cloud of dust and dirt.

After a moment of stunned silence, the crowd of spectators rushed toward the accident. They found both men under the plane, Selfridge under the engine. He suffered a skull fracture and died. Wright, seriously injured with a fractured thigh and ribs, recovered after a hospital stay.

Despite having one of its own men become America's first aircraft fatality, the Army was sufficiently impressed by Orville Wright's flight demonstration to purchase one Flyer airplane for $25,000.

FIRST AIRPLANE FLIGHT OFF A SHIP

The first airplane flight off a ship took place in Hampton Roads on November 14, 1910, when Eugene Ely flew a Curtiss biplane off a wooden ramp aboard the U.S. Navy scout cruiser *Birmingham* anchored off Old Point Comfort.

Ely, a civilian pilot associated with aviation pioneer Glenn Curtiss, had been approached by Navy captain Washington Irving Chambers during an air show in Baltimore about attempting to fly an airplane off the deck of a ship. Chambers, a leading Navy proponent of naval aviation, was considering the possibility of using aircraft as scouting instruments for battleships and cruisers.

Ely agreed to attempt the flight, and Chambers made arrangements to have the scout cruiser *Birmingham* enter the Norfolk Navy Yard to have her forecastle fitted with an 83-foot long wooden ramp, which sloped five degrees toward the bow.

On the morning of November 14, 1910, all was ready for the impending flight. Ely's plane was a four-cylinder engine Curtiss biplane, capable of making a speed of about sixty miles an hour.

The plane was hoisted aboard the *Birmingham*, which then headed slowly down the Elizabeth River into Hampton Roads escorted by the destroyers *Roe* and *Terry* and the torpedo boats *Bailey* and *Stringham*. The ships were to act as rescue stations in case the plane crashed into the water.

The original plan was for the *Birmingham* to steam out into the Chesapeake Bay and head the ship into the wind. The plane was to take off and fly to the Norfolk Navy Yard and land at the Marine parade ground. But intermittent rain and hail showers obscured the landmarks and forced the cruiser to anchor off Old Point Comfort to await improvement in the weather.

The weather cleared somewhat in the afternoon, and the *Birmingham* began heaving up its anchor. Ely donned his life jacket and climbed into the plane to test the engine. It worked fine. Ely idled the engine and waited anxiously for the ship to get underway.

But the anchor was slow in coming aboard, and the weather

again looked threatening. The impatient Ely decided he could wait no longer for the ship to start steaming into the wind. He restarted the engine, signaling for his mechanic to release the securing cable for the plane, and at 3:16 p.m., Ely made his takeoff.

The plane rolled down the ramp, but failed to be airborne before it dropped off the bow of the ship. Ely struggled with the plane's controls. Just as the wheels touched the water after a thirty-seven-foot drop, the engine responded and Ely was able to pull the plane safely into the air. However, the encounter with the water drenched the pilot and splintered both propeller tips.

Ely lost his bearing due to poor visibility, and now knowing how badly his plane was damaged, he decided to land at his first opportunity. Five minutes later he spotted open land and landed safely near some beach houses at Willoughby Spit. The length of his flight was about five miles.

Eugene Ely had become the first man to fly an airplane off the deck of a ship.

Two months later, on January 18, 1911, Ely again made history when he made the first airplane landing on a ship, the armored cruiser *Pennsylvania* in San Francisco harbor.

Eugene Ely made history on November 14, 1910, when he became the first man to fly an airplane off a ship. He flew a Curtiss biplane off the deck of the U.S. Navy scout cruiser Birmingham *anchored in Hampton Roads. Courtesy of the Hampton Roads Naval Museum*

Eugene Ely flies his Curtiss biplane off the ramp built on the forecastle of the U.S. Navy scout cruiser Birmingham. *This historic first flight took place when the* Birmingham *was anchored off Old Point Comfort in Hampton Roads. Courtesy of the Hampton Roads Naval Museum*

FIRST ARMY AERIAL PHOTOGRAPHY SCHOOL

When military aircraft were first used in World War I, they spawned the need for new equipment and new specialties by support personnel. Aerial photography became an important mission for military aircraft.

Using aircraft as a platform, photographers took pictures of enemy troop formations and installations. Aerial reconnaissance flights thus became important tools for troop commanders.

To meet the need for aerial photographers, the Army on October 23, 1917, established the first United States Army School of Aerial Photography at Langley Field in Hampton.

Sgt. M. A. McKinney, who was later promoted to captain, was the officer-in-charge. Before he entered the Army, McKinney had been a commercial photographer.

The first class of twelve "aero-photographers" graduated in late January 1918, and were immediately sent to France.

In mid-1918, the school was transferred to Rochester, New York.

Students at the Army School of Aerial Photography flew their training missions in the Curtiss JN-4 "Jenny" aircraft.

FIRST BATTLESHIP SUNK BY AIRCRAFT

On July 21, 1921, the ex-German battleship *Ostfriesland*, anchored in the Chesapeake Bay, was sunk by Army bombers flying from Langley Field in Hampton.

This first aerial bombing of a battleship was the result of a furious war of words among American generals and admirals who debated heatedly the relative value of aircraft and warships. The aircraft had proved its value in the land war of World War I, but it had yet to prove its importance in naval warfare.

Aircraft proponents, led by Brig. Gen. William "Billy" Mitchell, assistant chief of the U.S. Army's Air Service, claimed that airplanes would make naval ships, especially battleships, obsolete. Mitchell had already begun lobbying for a separate air arm with its own secretary, coequal to the secretaries of the Army and Navy. He went so far as to insist that air power was capable by itself of providing for the national defense. Armies he saw as useful only for occupying land conquered by planes.

After much discussion, the War Department and the Navy Department agreed to conduct joint aerial bombing exercises against

German naval ships turned over to the United States at the end of World War I. The target ships would be anchored in the Chesapeake Bay.

The tests began on June 21, 1921, when the submarine U-117 was sunk by three Naval Air Service flying boats in only sixteen minutes. On July 13, Army Air Service bombers sank the destroyer G-102 using twenty-five pound and three hundred pound bombs. The cruiser *Frankfort* was the target of bombs dropped by Army, Navy, and Marine Corps aircraft on July 18. The cruiser was heavily damaged, but remained afloat, only to be sunk later by time bombs.

The big event, the bombing of the *Ostfriesland* began on July 20, when Army bombers from Langley Field attacked the battleship with 230, 550, and 600-pound bombs. These armor-piercing bombs tore through the two upper decks, but failed to do any serious damage to the ship's vital parts. She remained afloat.

Army fliers launched another attack on July 21, when Capt. Walter R. Lawson, with a squadron of six Martin and one Handley-Page bomber, each dropped a two thousand pound bomb on the anchored battleship.

One of the bombs exploded in the water near the battleship's side, ripping up her seams, letting water rush into her hull. The other bombs caused tremendous explosions, and after twenty-five minutes of low altitude bombing, the battleship *Ostfriesland* turned turtle and sank.

The bombing tests on the German ships brought no conclusive results. The Navy felt that since the target ships were obsolete (the *Ostfriesland* having been completed in 1909), and having no heavy deck armor, the results were less than conclusive. Gen. Mitchell relentlessly pursued his allegations that air power was superior to armies and navies. His zeal led to a court martial and his dismissal from the service.

Mitchell's air power arguments eventually gained support. He had proven the vulnerability of the battleship to air attack, and the Navy took steps to build better and more heavily armed surface ships. The Army's Air Service became the U.S. Air Force, with a secretary ranked equal to the secretaries of the Army and Navy.

FIRST JET AIRCRAFT TO OPERATE FROM A CARRIER

The FD-1 Phantom jet fighter built by the McDonnell Corporation, St. Louis, Missouri, was the first jet-propelled aircraft

53

to operate from an aircraft carrier.

On July 21, 1946, Lt. Cdr. James Davidson, USN, piloted the first FD-1 Phantom jet fighter to land on and take off from the carrier USS *Franklin D. Roosevelt* (CV-42), operating off Cape Henry.

Davidson's trial flights, which included several take-offs and landings, proved the jet aircraft's adaptability to Navy carrier operations.

The single-seater FD-1 Phantom was built by McDonnell as a general purpose Navy-Marine Corps fighter. The plane first flew on January 26, 1945, but its introduction into the fleet was delayed by slow design progress.

The Phantom jet fighter had a wing span of forty feet, nine inches; length, thirty-eight feet nine inches; height, fourteen feet two inches.

Powered by two Westinghouse J30-WE-20 jet engines, the FD–1 attained a maximum speed of 410 knots and a service ceiling of 29,500 feet. It could climb 4,800 feet per minute. Its range was 670 nautical miles.

Armaments of the Phantom FD-1 fighter included four .50–caliber nose guns firing 1,300 rounds.

FIRST MILITARY HELIPORT

The world's first military heliport, Felker Field, was dedicated on December 7, 1954, at the U.S. Army Transportation Training Command, Fort Eustis.

The field was named after Warrant Officer Alfred C. Felker, who was killed in a helicopter accident near Wintersville, Georgia, on February 10, 1953, while on an extended cross-country flight.

Opening ceremonies featured an air show that demonstrated the comparative maneuverability of various types of helicopters and fixed-wing aircraft. Among the dignitaries attending the dedication ceremony were helicopter pioneer Igor Sikorsky and Maj. Gen. Paul F. Yount, Chief of Army Transportation.

Revolutionary in airfield construction, Felker Field was built as a huge circular taxiway divided into quarter sections by two 600-foot runways. Around the outer edge, extending from the circle like spokes of a wheel, were eight circular helicopter landing pads. A hangar, control tower, shop area and warehouse were part of the $1,000,000 heliport complex.

The original idea for the heliport was conceived in 1949 by Col.

William B. Bunker while serving as assistant to the Chief of Transportation for Army Aviation. The Transportation Corps was then given the responsibility for providing helicopter units for the tactical and logistical support of the armies. Fort Eustis, center of the Transportation Corps' training mission, was the logical site for the first heliport.

Felker Army Airfield, as it is now called, was later remodeled to comply with modern aviation requirements, including the installation of a ground control approach (GCA) radar system. The field now services both helicopters and fixed wing aircraft.

The world's first military heliport, Felker Field at Fort Eustis, became operational on December 7, 1954. Unique in design, it was shaped as a huge wheel. Courtesy of U.S. Army Transportation Center, Fort Eustis

FIRST TRAINING FOR FIRST ASTRONAUTS

On April 9, 1959, the National Aeronautics and Space Administration (NASA) in Washington, D. C., introduced to the world seven fliers selected to be America's first astronauts. On April 29, 1959, the seven astronauts attended their first training session conducted by the Space Task Group at NASA's Langley Research Center in Hampton.

Selected as astronauts for Project Mercury, the United States' first manned space project, were Lt. Malcolm Scott Carpenter, U.S. Navy; Capt. Leroy Gorden Cooper, U.S. Air Force; Lt. Col. John Herschel Glenn, U.S. Marine Corps; Lt. Virgil Ivan Grissom, U.S. Air Force; Lt. Cdr. Walter Marty Schirra, U.S. Navy; Lt. Cdr. Alan Bartlett Shepard, U.S. Navy; and Capt. Donald Kent Slayton, U.S. Air Force.

NASA originally reviewed the records of 508 Air Force, Navy, Marine, and Army pilots as possible candidates as astronauts for the mercury space program. The seven pilots chosen as America's first astronauts were picked from the final group of eighteen qualified candidates.

After two weeks of lectures at Langley, the group began to visit various technical, military, and medical centers, and the launch site at Cape Canaveral, Florida. Their training included mechanics and aerodynamics, principles of guidance and control, communications, physiology, and a course in star recognition and practical celestial navigation.

On May 5, 1961, the United States sent its first man into space when astronaut Alan B. Shepard was hurled into space by a Redstone rocket launched from Cape Canaveral. Shepard's flight in the space capsule *Freedom* lasted fifteen minutes, twenty-two seconds.

John Glenn became the first American astronaut to orbit the earth on February 20, 1962. His capsule *Friendship 7* was blased into space from Cape Canaveral by an Atlas-D rocket. Glenn orbited the earth three times, spending four hours, fifty-five minutes, twenty-three seconds in flight.

America's first seven astronauts received their first training at NASA's Langley Research Center in Hampton. Here the astronauts view configuration of Atlas booster and Mercury capsule. Seated, left to right, are Virgil Grissom, Malcolm Carpenter, Walter Slayton, and Leroy Cooper, Jr. Standing, left to right, Alan Shepard, Jr., Walter Schirra, and John Glenn, Jr. Courtesy of National Aeronautics and Space Administration

BOOKS

FIRST BOOKS

Printing of books, pamphlets, and newspapers was stifled during the early days of the Virginia colony. The upper-class colonists looked down on printing and publishing as a grubby business, and the political leaders took a dim view of permitting anything to get into print except their official communications.

The ruling-class opposition to the printed word was forcibly expressed by Virginia's reactionary governor, Sir William Berkeley, who wrote to his government in England in 1671: "But, I thank God, there are no free schools nor printing, and I hope we shall not have these hundred years; for learning has brought disobedience, and heresy, and sects into the world, and printing has divulged them, and libels against the best government. God keep us from both!"

It was Virginia's good fortune that William Parks, a public printer at Annapolis, Maryland, decided to enlarge his business in 1730, and open a new shop on Duke of Gloucester Street in Williamsburg. Parks not only became the first public printer in Virginia, but he also published Virginia's first newspaper, *The Virginia Gazette*, and began publishing a variety of books, many of which were the first of their kind in America. Some of his publications were forerunners of the current vogue of "how to" best-sellers.

William Parks was born in Ludlow, England, about 1698. He is credited with establishing the first presses in his native town, and starting the first newspapers in Ludlow and Reading.

In early 1725, he came to America, settling first in Annapolis, where he became a public printer and established the newspaper, *Maryland Gazette*.

One of William Parks' earliest books published in Williamsburg was John Markland's *Typographia. An Ode, on Printing.* This was the first printed publications about printing in America. In the book, issued in 1730, Markland rejoiced over the establishment of a printing press in Virginia.

Also in 1730, Parks published *The Dealers' Pocket Companion,* the first handbook of rates and tables for use in buying and selling tobacco.

In 1734, Parks printed the first American book on sports, *A Compleat System of Fencing: or The Act of Defence, in the Use of the Small-Sword* by Edward Blackwell. The book's title page declared that it was "chiefly for gentlemen, promoters, and lovers of that science in North America." It was based on a fencing book published in London in 1705.

One of William Parks' best-sellers was the first American book on the art of cookery printed in 1742. The book, *The Compleat Housewife: Or, Accomplished Gentlewomen's Companion,* was a compilation of recipes from a much larger volume written by Mrs. E. Smith of London. The book published by Parks omitted recipes containing ingredients not to be found in Virginia. The cookbook was proclaimed to have a collection of "the most approved Receipts...never before made Publick, in these Parts; fit either for private Families, or such Publick-Spirited Gentlewomen as would be beneficent to their poor Neighbors."

FIRST REGIONAL COOKBOOK

The Virginia Housewife, written by Mary Randolph, was the first regional cookbook published in America. It was printed in 1824 by Davis and Force, a firm located on Pennsylvania Avenue in Washington, D. C.

Mary Randolph, born in 1762 at Ampthill on the James River, was married to her second cousin, David Meade Randolph of Curles. David was a Federalist who served as United States Marshal under presidents George Washington and John Adams. They lived in a large house in Richmond where they entertained lavishly.

When Thomas Jefferson became president, David Randolph lost his Federal appointment, and the Randolph's financial situation became so critical that they had to sell their home and move into a rented house. Determined not to buckle under, Mary Randolph established a boarding house on Cary Street in Richmond.

Her food and accommodations were highly acclaimed. Mrs.

Randolph brought personal flair to her cookery, earning her the reputation of Virginia's best cook.

Late in 1819, Mary and her husband moved to Washington, D. C., where they lived with their son William. Unaccustomed to the leisure she found in the nation's capital, Mary Randolph began to gather the fruits of her years of successful housekeeping into a cookbook.

In her preface, Mary Randolph recounts the inception of the book:

"The difficulties I encountered when I first entered on the duties of a House-keeping life, from the want of books sufficiently clear and concise, to impart knowledge to a Tyro, compelled me to study the subject, and by actual experiment to reduce everything to proper weights and measures. This method I found not only to diminish the necessary attention and labor but to be also economical; for when the ingredients employed were given just proportions, the article made was always good."

She stressed the need for good household management, and suggested that every lady reader spend an hour each morning planning domestic tasks and thus avoid the "horrible drudgery of keeping house."

Mrs. Randolph included recipes for dishes that have remained southern favorites, such as "toasting (boiling and baking) a ham;" stuffing a ham; baking, roasting and broiling shad; boiling turnip tops "with bacon in the Virginia style;" sweet potato pudding; cornmeal bread; batter cakes; and batter bread.

Among Mary Randolph's recipes were instructions for making catfish soup, which she called "an excellent Dish for those who have not imbided a needless prejudice against those delicious Fish." She also provided a recipe for curing and preparing 150 pounds of beef, and instructions how to "collar a calf's head."

Mrs. Randolph offered no short cuts in her cooking instructions. Calling her book a "method in the soul of management," she stressed that the quality of prepared food, not its great variety, was important. "Profusion is not elegance," she wrote.

Despite difficulties in having it published, *The Virginia Housewife* was an immediate success. A second edition was published in 1825. By 1850, eleven editions had been published, and after expiration of the copyright, reprints have been issued periodically, the latest version in the mid-1980s.

The success of *The Virginia Housewife* led publishers to issue cookbooks for other regions of America.

COMMUNICATIONS

FIRST WIRELESS TELEGRAPHY

In 1896, Gugliemo Marconi was credited with developing the first wireless telegraphy, but in October 1866, eight years before Marconi was born, the first successful demonstration of "aerial telegraphy" took place in Virginia's Blue Ridge Mountains.

Mahlon Loomis, a dentist practicing in Washington, D. C., who also resided in Lynchburg, made the world's first radio transmission when he succeeded in transmitting wireless signals over a distance of fourteen miles between Catochon Mountain and Beorse Deer Mountain in Loudoun County. His experiment was witnessed by prominent scientists and electricians, and by at least two members of the U.S. Congress.

From each of the two mountain peaks, Dr. Loomis let fly a kite attached to a six hundred-foot-long copper wire. Each wire was connected to a galvanometer (indicator of electric current) and then grounded in a pool of water. Alternately making and breaking the connection of one galvanometer with its kite wire, the needle at the other galvanometer moved, providing Loomis with the first wireless telegraphed "messages." Loomis continued his experiment for about three hours, repeating the transmission of signals from one mountain peak to the other mountain every five minutes.

Out of his experiments, Loomis believed that the earth was surrounded by an "aura" which he termed as a "static sea." This "static sea" would enable man to send wireless messages over unlimited distances, Loomis theorized. Once he proposed sending wireless messages between America and Europe.

Dr. Loomis was unsuccessful in obtaining financial backing necessary to develop his wireless experiments.

Loomis's experiments did attract the attention of several

Senators and Congressmen, who introduced a bill to incorporate the Loomis Aerial Telegraph Company. It would grant an appropriation of $50,000 to perfect his discovery, and enable him to work toward transmitting wireless messages from the United States to Europe. When Pres. Grant signed the legislation in 1873, however, it restricted the company's corporate powers to the District of Columbia. Unable to operate elsewhere, the Loomis Aerial Telegraph Company never got started.

Loomis did, however, have the satisfaction of having the United States Patent Office issue him a patent for the "Improvement of Telegraphing." Issued on July 30, 1872, it was the first U.S. patent ever granted for a system of wireless telegraphy.

Just before Dr. Mahlon Loomis died in 1886 at the age of sixty, he told his brother George that he was right about sending wireless messages, "I shall never see it perfected, but it will be, and others will have the honor of the discovery."

FIRST CITY TO ADVERTISE ON NATIONAL TV TO ATTRACT RETAILERS

Portsmouth became the first city in the nation to go on nationwide television to attract new retailers when its 60-second commercial was aired September 2, 1986, on Cable News Network (CNN).

The TV spot, "The Right Place, The Right Time," shown on the CNN program "Crossfire," called attention to business opportunities in Virginia's "newest boom town"—Portsmouth.

The city's Economic Development Department received more than fifteen hundred telephoned responses to its initial national TV campaign to attract new businesses. The campaign was considered a success.

The TV campaign and a follow-up print media advertising campaign to attract retailers to Portsmouth was developed by Primm and Company of Norfolk. Both campaigns were sponsored by the Portsmouth Partnership, a coalition of business, civic and political leaders formed in 1983 as a program of the Hampton Roads Chamber of Commerce/Portsmouth to support economic and community development.

The Right Place
Portsmouth
The Right Time

This is the print media version of Portsmouth's TV spot, "The Right Place, The Right Time." The television commercial was the first used by a city to attract new retailers. Courtesy of Primm and Company

COMMUNITY SERVICES

FIRST HIGHWAY POST OFFICE

The first Highway Post Office service was established February 10, 1941, when an especially equipped U.S. Post Office Department bus began carrying mail between Washington, D. C. and Harrisonburg. The first Highway Post Office was equipped with facilities for sorting, handling and dispatching mail in a manner similar to that performed in standard railway postal cars. The 146-mile route between Washington and Harrisonburg served 22 intermediate post offices.

The Highway Post Office service was established to supplement the Railway Mail Service that had declined as more and more passenger trains were eliminated.

The initial trip of the Highway Post Office left Washington, D. C. at 5:30 a.m., February 10, 1941, and arrived at its destination, the Post Office at Harrisonburg, at 11:00 a.m. HPO No. 1 was greeted in Harrisonburg by about five hundred persons, led by Postmaster G. Fred Switzer.

At each stop along its route, HPO No. 1 was met by a crowd of enthusiastic well wishers. At Woodstock, the county seat of Shenandoah County, more than two thousand persons, many of them school children, turned out to greet HPO No. 1 when it arrived at 9:41 a.m. Despite the eager crowd, HPO No. 1 kept its schedule, departing promptly at 9:46 a.m.

HPO No. 1 began the return trip from Harrisonburg at 4:00 p.m., arriving in Washington at 9:20 p.m.

The crew on the first trip of Highway Post Office No. 1 consisted of Clyde C. Peters, Claude M. Dellinger, Lovell H. Crove, and Orville R. Linskey. Peters was Clerk-in-Charge, and the driver was Henry L.

Naylor. The postal workers handled a total of 114,311 pieces of mail for the round trip of HPO No. 1.

The Highway Post Office service grew until it reached its zenith of more than two hundred routes across the country, but on June 30, 1974 it ended, halted by advancing technology and the big city lure that shrank the small towns it served faithfully for thirty-three years. The first Highway Post Office service between Washington, D. C. and Harrisonburg ended in 1965.

Mail bags are being taken from the first Highway Post Office, which made its initial run from Washington, D. C. to Harrisonburg on February 10, 1941. Courtesy of the U.S. Postal Service

Postmaster General Frank Walker helps President Franklin D. Roosevelt post the first letter aboard Highway Post Office No. 1. Courtesy of the Smithsonian Institution

Postal workers sort mail in transit aboard the nation's first Highway Post Office. Courtesy of the U.S. Postal Service

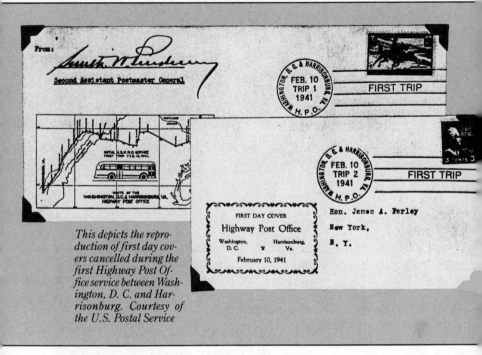

This depicts the reproduction of first day covers cancelled during the first Highway Post Office service between Washington, D. C. and Harrisonburg. Courtesy of the U.S. Postal Service

FIRST WOMAN FIRE DEPARTMENT BATTALION CHIEF

Donna Pratt Brehm became the first female battalion chief of a major U.S. metropolitan fire department when she was sworn in as a battalion chief in the Virginia Beach Fire Department on December 31, 1985.

Upon her promotion, Mrs. Brehm was assigned to the fire department's training center as an assistant program manager, responsible for safety programs and proficiency tests for firefighters.

Mrs. Brehm began her firefighting career as a volunteer. Her husband Robert Brehm, another volunteer with the Virginia Beach Fire Department, was promoted to battalion chief in October 1984. With the promotion of Mrs. Brehm, the Virginia Beach Fire Department appeared to be the only fire department in the country with a husband-and-wife team of battalion chiefs.

Another honor was bestowed upon Donna Brehm when the local American Legion chapter named her as Virginia Beach "Firefighter of the Year 1985."

Donna Brehm, Virginia Beach Fire Department, was the first female battalion chief of a major U.S. metropolitan fire department. Courtesy of the Office of Public Information, City of Virginia Beach

FIRST FACILITY FOR REMOVING RESIDUAL SOLIDS FROM WATER

The nation's first facility for removing residual solids from treated water began operating February 15, 1987, at the City of Norfolk's Moores Bridges Water Treatment Plant. The facility is operated by the Division of Water Production in the city's Utilities Department.

The special equipment removes solids that normally remain after the water undergoes purification treatment. Treated solids, which are usually high in metallic content, pass through a diaphragm filter press and emit in small sheets. These sheets are then removed and trucked to a landfill in Suffolk.

The residual solids removal equipment was manufactured by Envirex Inc., Waukesha, Wisconsin.

CRIME

FIRST KIDNAPPING

The first recorded case of kidnapping in America took place in the spring of 1613 when Capt. Samuel Argall kidnapped the Indian princess Pocahontas, holding her for ransom at an Indian village called Petomek, in what is now Stafford County. The Potomac River takes its name from this Indian village.

Captain Argall had sailed his ship out of Jamestown up to the Potomac River where he explored the area and sought trade with the Indians. When he learned that Pocahontas was in the area, Argall persuaded Iapassus, a local Indian chief, to betray Pocahontas and lure her aboard his ship.

Iapassus got his wife to bring Pocahontas down to the shore, where she feigned a desire to see the ship. Iapassus said it was not proper for a woman to go aboard a ship alone, so the wife pleaded with Pocahontas to go with her. Pocahontas agreed. The three were welcomed aboard by Capt. Argall, who offered his "guests" a supper.

After the meal, Argall kept Pocahontas under guard in his cabin and set Iapassus and his wife ashore with a copper pot as payment for their treachery. Then he dispatched an Indian runner to the Algonquin Indian Chief Powhatan, telling him that his daughter was held hostage and would be freed only if Powhatan returned captured Englishmen, their arms and tools, and provided the British with great quantity of corn.

Powhatan sent word that he would agree to Argall's demand, and asked that his daughter be treated well.

Instead of sailing further up the Potomac River to Powhatan's camp, Argall returned to Jamestown with his famous hostage.

Pocahontas was not to be reunited with her Indian family,

instead she would remain at Jamestown as a guest of the governor rather than as a prisoner.

FIRST LYNCH LAW

The first "Lynch Law" had nothing to do with lynching, an illegal hanging, but was an attempt by a Virginia patriot to maintain law and order during a time of prevailing lawlessness.

During the disorganized conditions which accompanied the American Revolution, Charles Lynch, a justice of peace, took charge of law and order by presiding over an unofficial court in Bedford County.

He invoked what could be termed martial law to check the activities of horse thieves and other criminals, and Tories who were accused of aiding the British.

Lynch was a firm man. While his rump court was unlawful, the trials were carried out in the usual legal forms. The most severe sentences issued by the Lynch court were fines and floggings. Many persons accused of minor crimes were paroled on their word. Tories were often released once they swore allegiance to support the Revolution.

In 1782, the Virginia Legislature decided that Lynch's sentencing of criminals and Tory conspirators had been justified because of imminent danger to the state during the Revolution and exonerated him.

But because Charles Lynch meted out unofficial justice, his name is today associated with the term, "lynch law," describing mob courts, and "lynchings," hangings without any trial at all.

EDUCATION

FIRST FREE SCHOOL

The first educational endowment for establishing the first free school in America was created by the will of Benjamin Syms, an Isle of Wight planter who died in February 1635.

Farmer Syms, an illiterate, who signed his will with an "X," donated two hundred acres of land on the Poquoson River and eight cows "for the maintenance of a learned or honest man to keep upon said grounds a free school."

America's first free school was established for the children of Elizabeth City (now Hampton) and Poquoson parishes. The Syms free school may have been located on what is now the Langley Air Force Base.

The teacher was paid with money collected from the sale of milk and the calves produced by the original herd of eight cows.

FIRST PHI BETA KAPPA SOCIETY

America's first Greek letter fraternity, the Phi Beta Kappa, began on December 5, 1776, with a meeting of five students from the College of William and Mary in the Raleigh Tavern at Williamsburg.

Present at the initial meeting of the fraternity in the Apollo Room of the Raleigh Tavern were John Smith, an eighteen-year-old from Northumberland, Thomas Smith, as well as Richard Booker, Armistead Smith, and John Jones.

The first action of the idealist students was to approve the Greek phrase meaning, "love of wisdom the guide of life," the initials of which gave the society its name. Aims of the fraternity would be to promote friendship, morality, and literature.

Soon other William and Mary students were invited to join the Phi Beta Kappa. Its members met frequently to debate the issues of the day: slavery, church and state, and the dangers of a standing army.

Today the Phi Beta Kappa is the most prestigious U.S. honor society for college and university students in the liberal arts and sciences.

FIRST STATE-SUPPORTED LOTTERY FOR HIGHER EDUCATION

The Virginia General Assembly on June 21, 1777, approved the nation's first state-supported lottery for higher education. The lottery would raise $4,200 to finance construction of new buildings for the Hampden-Sydney College in Prince Edward Country.

Hampden-Sydney College was formally organized in February 1775 as the first college in Virginia affiliated with the Presbyterian Church. Students and faculty began gathering in the fall of 1775, although the official opening of the college was delayed until January 1, 1776. The College has been in continuous operation since its opening. Today the liberal arts college of eight hundred students is the oldest of the country's few remaining all-male colleges.

Money for education was hard to come by during the American Revolution, so, on April 11, 1777, the college's Board of Trustees appointed a committee to draw up a scheme for conducting a lottery to raise funds to erect additional buildings. The committee's plan was approved by the Virginia General Assembly, and the lottery managers advertised the lottery plan in the *Virginia Gazette* on July 4, 1777.

The lottery was to raise $4,200 (or 1,260 pounds) to finance the construction of buildings. The college was to sell 5,600 tickets at five dollars each. Of the total number of tickets, 2,483 would be drawn for prizes, ranging from one $2,000 prize to 1,310 prizes of five dollars each. Total prizes would value $28,000, and the college would get its share by deducting 15 percent of each prize, to yield $4,200.

While the lottery managers were enthused about their fund-raising project, the public apparently was not eager to buy tickets of chance. As late as March 1783, the president of the college was beseeching the lottery managers to settle their accounts "as speedily as possible."

The educational-inspired lottery failed, but the college survived.

The Corps of Cadets are shown here drilling on the parade grounds of the Virginia Military Institute at Lexington. VMI is the nation's first state-supported military school. Courtesy of the Virginia Military Institute

FIRST STATE-SUPPORTED MILITARY SCHOOL

On November 11, 1839, twenty-three young Virginians were mustered into the service of the Commonwealth of Virginia to form the first Corps of Cadets at the Virginia Military Institute at Lexington. This first state-supported military school in the United States was established at the site of the Lexington Arsenal, which had been built in 1816 as the storage point of arms for the western part of Virginia.

Lexington's leading citizens, led by a young attorney, John Thomas Lewis Preston (later Colonel), proposed that the arsenal be transformed into a military college, with students protecting the arms there while pursuing educational courses. The Virginia General Assembly passed an act on March 29, 1839, authorizing the establishment of the Virginia Military Institute.

Professor (later Major General) Francis Henney Smith, a distinguished 1833 graduate from the United States Military Academy at West Point, New York, was named the first Superintendent of VMI and presided over the affairs of the Institute for fifty years.

Civil engineering, a subject rarely taught in colleges and universities before 1839, was established at the founding of VMI as the cornerstone of its program. The first industrial chemistry course in the south was offered at VMI, and, in 1868, modern courses in physics and meteorology were developed by Commodore Matthew Fontaine Maury.

Today VMI is a fully accredited state-supported undergraduate college for young men. It offers a choice of majors from the general fields of engineering, liberal arts, and the sciences.

All students are members of the Corps of Cadets. In addition, all participate in officer training programs associated with Army, Naval, or Air Force ROTC.

The VMI program is not specifically designed to produce officers for the armed forces, but rather is based on the citizen-soldier concept, wherein a man is prepared to take his place in civilian life but ready to respond in times of national military need.

Among the VMI teachers in the early years was a professor of "natural philosophy"—physics, as it is called today—named Professor Thomas Jonathan Jackson. With the outbreak of the Civil War, the professor, later to win fame as Gen. "Stonewall" Jackson, trained cadets to serve with the Confederate Army in the Richmond area. The Corps of Cadets was called into service a number of times during the Civil War.

On May 15, 1864, an engagement took place at New Market in the Shenandoah Valley that brought renown to the cadets of the Virginia Military Institute. Called upon by Confederate Gen. John C. Breckinridge to bolster the southern line against the advancing troops of Union Gen. Franz Sigel, some 240 young men of the Corps of Cadets marched into battle alongside seasoned Confederate soldiers. They charged gallantly and won credit for helping turn the tide in favor of the Confederate forces. The toll: ten cadets killed and forty-seven wounded. Six of the dead are buried under the New Market monument on the VMI grounds. Each year on May 15 the Corps of Cadets pay tribute to the courage of the New Market cadets in formal ceremonies held at the Institute.

In World War I, the Virginia Military Institute gave 1,830 trained men to the U.S. armed forces. In World War II, the number was 4,100 including sixty-two officers of general or flag rank. The most illustrious of these was General of the Army George C. Marshall.

While a military school, historically, only about 15 percent of VMI's graduates have chosen military careers. Most graduates enter finance, business, industry, government service, and the professions.

FIRST FULLY STATE-SUPPORTED BLACK COLLEGE

On Monday, October 1, 1883, sixty-two students attended opening classes of America's first fully state-supported black college, the Virginia Normal and Collegiate Institute in Ettrick, a suburb of Petersburg. Today this educational institution is known as the Virginia State University.

While there had been other black colleges established in the nation before the Civil War, and while a few states had provided piddling amounts of funding to black schools, the Commonwealth of Virginia was the first state to provide large amounts of funding for both construction and yearly operations of a black college.

Virginia State University was founded on March 6, 1882, when the Virginia legislature passed a bill to charter the Virginia Normal and Collegiate Institute. The bill was sponsored by Delegate Alfred W. Harris, a black attorney with offices in Petersburg who lived in and represented Dinwiddie County in the General Assembly.

The political climate was favorable to black education at this time. Harris was able to persuade a majority of the legislators that the institute should have a black faculty and six blacks of the seven-member board of visitors. There was some sentiment at the time for having whites operate the school and provide instruction.

The bill also provided $100,000 from railroad bonds to buy a school site and erect the main building. A $20,000 annual appropriation was included for operation. The top faculty salary was set at $1,500 a year.

Virginia Normal and Collegiate Institute thus became the first fully state-supported black college in America. The curriculum initially provided for three-year normal (teacher training) and four-year bachelor's degree programs.

Eight students became the first graduates of VNCI's Normal Department in 1886. They were: Carrie Bragg, Lucretia Campbell, James Shields, and Fannie R. Walker from Petersburg; Susie B. Douglas of Alexandria; Jerry F. Lucas of Manassas; William H. Davis of Chatham; and Robert W. Green of Charlottesville.

The first bachelor's degree was awarded in 1889 to Walter Fayerman of Petersburg. He later became a physician.

The year 1902 brought difficulties to Virginia blacks. The state's new constitution took effect, and blacks lost the right to vote. The Virginia Assembly changed the mission and name of VNCI by passing a new charter law. The school was renamed Virginia Normal and Industrial Institute, and bachelor's degrees were abolished. Baccalaureate programs would not resume until two decades later.

In 1930, the Virginia Legislature again amended the charter act and changed the school's name to Virginia State College for Negroes.

In 1946, the Virginia Legislature amended the charter law to change the school's name to Virginia State College, dropping the "for Negroes" part of the name.

The school's campaign to gain university status succeeded in 1979 when the Virginia Assembly passed a law renaming the school Virginia State University, and stressing that it would become the regional university for all residents of southside Virginia.

Today Virginia State University is a highly respected institution of higher learning in the Commonwealth of Virginia with a student body of four thousand students.

Old Virginia Hall, the main building of the Virginia Normal and Collegiate Institute (now Virginia State University), was started in 1883, completed in 1888, and torn down in the 1930s to make way for the present Virginia Hall. First classes of VNCI began on October 1, 1883, in a large plantation house on the Fleets Farm in the village of Ettrick, now a suburb of Petersburg. Courtesy of Virginia State University

This historic photo-graph shows three faculty members and the first eight students to graduate from Virginia Normal and Collegiate Institute in 1886. Front row, left to right, are VNCI President John M. Langston, Robert W. Green (student), Mrs. Ida R. Harris (faculty), and Professor James M. Colson. Rear row, left to right students James Shields, Lucretia Campbell, Susie B. Douglas, Fannie R. Walker, Carrie Bragg, William H. Davis, and Jerry F. Lucas. Courtesy of Virginia State University

FIRST COLLEGE TO TEACH PHYSICAL EDUCATION

The first physical education course taught at an American college began in the autumn of 1887 at Randolph Macon College in Ashland.

The physical education program, which consisted mainly of calisthenics, was taught by Professor J. B. Crenshaw, and was an outgrowth of the college's course in hygiene.

Morals rather than athletics were the motives for the physical education course. College president William W. Bennett gave three reasons for "a regular system of physical training."

First, "physical exercise in company is the physician's preventive and remedy for the terrible vice of masturbation which wrecks more minds and bodies than probably any other one cause of ruin among youths outwardly moral."

Second, the exercise would give the students greater control over their bodies to "bring it under full control of the will for life's purposes."

Third, to develop "a desirable College spirit."

FIRST NAVY MUSIC SCHOOL

The U.S. Navy's first school for musicians was established in 1902 at the small Saint Helena Receiving Station in the Berkley section of Norfolk.

By the time of the Civil War there were bands on the larger ships of the United States fleet, but the Navy had no central place from which to enlist, assemble, and train musicians for fleet bands.

The St. Helena Receiving Station consisted of a parade ground, and less than a dozen buildings. Most of the operations of the station were carried out on board two decommissioned frigates, the *Richmond* and *Franklin*, which permanently tied up at St. Helena. The *Richmond* was later converted to quarters for the commanding officer.

Each evening, except on Sundays, a Navy orchestra would present a concert aboard the *Richmond* for the benefit of the commanding officer, as well as the general public.

The first Navy Music School was housed in a group of small shed-type buildings, mostly for storage of instruments, and a great deal of the playing was done out of doors. As the need became greater, a large space was found over a sail shop at the station.

Bandmaster Thomas Kennedy, the first leader of the first Navy Music School, auditioned musicians to serve as bandsmen in the fleet. Actually there was very little training at this school. Usually the musicians enlisted formed into musical groups and shipped aboard the many ships requesting bands.

Complete bands were sent the first year of the school to the battleships *Maine* and *Texas*. Seventeen musicians under Bandmaster P. DeSantis were ordered from St. Helena to the U.S. Naval Academy in Annapolis, Maryland, to augment the then civilian band.

Most musicians who enlisted in the Navy were fairly accomplished in their art, but there were also men who needed help by instructors. If a student was not proficient in a certain instrument, he was allowed to try other instruments in hope that he might find one that was "a natural."

During this period, musicians were allowed to enlist in the Navy under two different programs. First, if a man enlisted as an apprentice seaman and didn't qualify on an instrument, he was retained in the Navy as a regular seaman. However, if he enlisted as a landsman apprentice and failed to make the grade, his enlistment was terminated and he returned to civilian life.

After the Navy built a Naval Operating Base in Norfolk in 1917, the Navy Music School was moved to a new location at the base.

It was not until 1935 that the Navy set up a formal training program for musicians by establishing the Navy School of Music at the Navy Yard in Washington, D. C. In 1964, the Navy School of Music was relocated to the Naval Amphibious Base in Little Creek, Norfolk. The school now provides instruction to approximately eight hundred musicians from the Navy, Marine Corps, and Army.

EXPLORATIONS

FIRST LANDING OF PERMANENT SETTLERS

The first landing of permanent British settlers in America took place on April 26, 1607, with the arrival of the vessels *Susan Constant, Godspeed*, and *Discovery* on the south side of the entrance to Chesapeake Bay. The first settlers named their landing site Cape Henry in honor of the Prince of Wales.

The three-ship fleet, under the command of Capt. Christopher Newport in the 100-ton flagship *Susan Constant*, had left London, England, on December 20, 1606. The *Godspeed*, forty tons, was commanded by Capt. Bartholomew Gosnold; the 20-ton *Discovery* was skippered by Capt. Edward Maria Wingfield.

On board the three ships were 104 men who were being sent to Virginia to establish the first "plantation and habitation" under the auspices of the London Company, a private corporation established by a charter granted by King James I.

After encountering delaying winter storms off the English coast, the voyagers sailed across the Atlantic Ocean with stops at the Canary Islands and the West Indies before finally anchoring off Virginia shores about four o'clock in the morning of April 26, 1607.

The first settlers probably cast their anchors in Virginia waters some two or three miles westward of the present location of the Old Cape Henry Lighthouse, within the Chesapeake Bay, and nearly on a south line with the inland waters of what is now known as Broad Bay, and its adjoining waters, known as Lynnhaven Bay.

Capt. Newport led a party of twenty men ashore to explore the region. The first sight of land was dazzling to the sea-weary eyes. One member of the landing party, Capt. George S. Percy, later wrote in his diary of "faire meadowes and goodly tall Trees with such Freshwaters running through the woods, as I was ravished at the first sight thereof."

Upon returning to their ships that evening, the explorers were attacked by Indians who wounded Capt. Gabriel Archer and a sailor named Mather Morton. The Indians withdrew into the woods when fired upon by the British.

On the third day, April 28, 1607, the British explorers assembled and launched a flat-bottomed shallop which they had brought with them. Capt. Newport led a party up to what is now Hampton Roads and found lands they named Willoughby Spit and Cape Comfort (now known as Old Point Comfort).

On April 29, 1607, the British adventurers erected a wooden cross on the sand dunes at their landing site and named it Cape Henry.

The next day, they left Cape Henry and sailed toward Cape Comfort and then up the James River in search of a permanent settlement place. After considering numerous locations, they picked the site of Jamestown, where they arrived on May 13, 1607.

The First Landing Cross at Cape Henry marks the spot where America's first permanent English settlers, the Jamestown colonists, first touched the shores of the New World on April 26, 1607. The white stone cross was erected April 26, 1935, by the National Society, Daughters of the American Colonists. Seen in the background, at right, stands the Old Cape Henry Lighthouse, which became operative in 1792. To the left, the new Cape Henry Lighthouse, completed in 1881, is still operating. Courtesy of the City of Virginia Beach Tourist Development Division

Moored at Jamestown Festival Park are full-size reproductions of the three ships, the Godspeed, Susan Constant, and Discovery, which transported the first permanent British settlers to Virginia in 1607. The tiny ships sailed from London in December 1606, with 144 men and boys, most of them ill-equipped for life in the untamed wilderness. Only 104 were left when the ships made their first landing at what is now Cape Henry on April 26, 1607. Courtesy of the Virginia Division of Tourism

FIRST SCIENTIFIC EXPEDITION
SPONSORED BY THE U.S. GOVERNMENT

On the afternoon of August 18, 1838, six naval ships of the United States Exploring Expedition, under the command of Lt. Charles Wilkes, sailed out of Norfolk on the most extensive American scientific expedition of the nineteenth century. This first scientific expedition to be fitted out by the U.S. government, was authorized by Congress, which on May 14, 1836, appropriated $150,000 for the expedition to obtain navigational, oceanographic, geographic, and other scientific information from the Pacific.

Lt. Wilkes, who earlier had been chief of the U.S. Navy's Depot of Charts and Instruments, was in command of the flagship *Vincennes*, a sloop of war. Other ships of the Exploring Expedition were the sloop *Peacock*, the brig *Porpoise*, schooners *Sea Gull* and *Flying Fish*, and the store ship *Relief*.

Among the scientists assigned to the Exploring Expedition were famed geologist James Dana and conchologist Joseph Couthouy. Two leading artists of the day, Thomas Agate and John Drayton, went along to depict the Expedition's scientific finds.

After sailing out of Hampton Roads, the U.S. Exploring Expedition proceeded south from Cape Horn to the Antarctic continent. Later the squadron went to Australia, returning to Antarctica to chart and survey along the ice barrier. The Expedition criss-crossed the Pacific Ocean from the Sandwich (Hawaiian) Islands to the Philippines. It also explored and charted the northwest coast of America.

The rigors of the Expedition's long journey took its toll of men and ships. Some men deserted, others were killed in fights with Pacific island natives, and the entire crew of the schooner *Sea Gull* was lost when she foundered in a storm near Cape Horn.

The mission ended June 10, 1842, when Wilkes sailed into New York harbor with but two ships.

Wilkes and his men surveyed 280 islands, and mapped 800 miles of streams and coastlines in Oregon and 1,500 miles of the Antarctic coastal region. Thousands of zoological specimens were brought back to the United States. The reports and specimens obtained by the U.S. Exploring Expedition provided American scientists with volumes of information on the Pacific Ocean areas.

FINANCE

FIRST FEMALE BANK PRESIDENT

Maggie Lena Walker, the daughter of former slaves, became the first woman bank president in the United States when the St. Luke Penny Bank, which she founded, was incorporated in Richmond on July 28, 1903.

Mrs. Walker, an unusually gifted woman, was a driving force in the Independent Order of St. Luke, a fraternal insurance society established in Baltimore in 1867 by an ex-slave, Mary Prout, to minister to sick and elderly members, and to promote humanitarian causes among Negroes. Maggie Walker had joined the fraternal order when she was fourteen years of age.

Maggie Walker was born July 15, 1867, in Richmond to Elizabeth Draper, a former kitchen slave, then a cook in the home of Elizabeth Van Lew, a wealthy spinster and Union sympathizer. In 1868, her mother married William Mitchell, a butler in the same household.

The early death of Mitchell forced his widow to take in laundry in their small cottage. Maggie delivered the clothes and cared for her brother.

Maggie received her public education at the Lancaster School and in 1883 she graduated from Richmond's Armstrong Normal School. She then taught at Lancaster for three years.

In 1886, Maggie married Armstead Walker, Jr., a building contractor. They had two sons. Armstead died in 1915 leaving Maggie to manage a very large house and family.

As a member of the Independent Order of St. Luke, Maggie Walker served in numerous capacities of increasing responsibility. She became a member of the Order's Committee of Grand Chiefs, and served as the Grand Secretary. She improved the Order's endowment system; made the Order solvent, reversing a deteriorating financial condition; and established the St. Luke *Herald*, a newspaper to provide closer communication between the Order and the public. She also helped to start the St. Luke Emporium, a retail store.

Maggie Walker tirelessly preached the gospel of thrift, and when the St. Luke Penny Bank was established in 1903 with her as president, she encouraged children to establish savings accounts. Their deposits, no matter how small, were accepted. The bank's first day's deposits, exceeded eight thousand dollars. Soon more than twenty thousand black children had accounts in the Penny Bank.

Maggie served as the bank's president until 1931, when the bank merged with other Negro banks to form the Consolidated Bank and Trust Company, as it is known today. She served as chairman of the board of directors of the new bank until her death.

In addition to the numerous commitments she undertook on behalf of St. Luke, Maggie Walker was an advocate of black women's rights and served on the boards of trustees for several women's groups. She helped organize and served as vice president of the Richmond chapter of the National Association for the Advancement of Colored People.

A debilitating leg and knee injury in 1928 confined her to a wheelchair until her death of diabetic gangrene December 15, 1934.

Maggie Walker's home, a two-story, red brick house located at 110½ East Leigh Street in Richmond is now a National Historic Site administered by the National Park Service.

Maggie Lena Walker in 1903 became the first woman to be president of a bank, the St. Luke Penny Bank in Richmond. Courtesy of the National Park Service

The home of Maggie L. Walker at 110 ½ East Leigh Street, Richmond, is a National Historic Site. Courtesy of the National Park Service

GOVERNMENT

FIRST DEMOCRATIC ELECTION

The first democratic election in America took place at Cape Henry on April 26, 1607, when the first permanent British settlers voted to elect the president of their council.

Capt. Christopher Newport commanded the three-ship fleet of *Susan Constant, Godspeed,* and *Discovery* which brought the first 104 permanent British settlers to America. A new leader would be named upon reaching their destination.

When the ships arrived safely in Virginia, the settlers were to open a sealed box which contained instructions from King James's Council on how to conduct their assigned task in the New World.

The box was opened in the evening of April 26th after a landing party had explored the surrounding area. It contained, among other things, the names of the seven councilors who were to be in charge of the colony which would be established May 13, 1607, at Jamestown.

Named to the Colonial Council were Capt. Christopher Newport, Capt. Bartholomew Gosnold, Capt. Edward Maria Wingfield, Capt. John Smith, Capt. John Ratcliffe, Capt. John Martin, and Capt. George Kendall.

The royal failure to name a leader for the colony provided the Council members with their first exercise in democracy—election.

They chose Wingfield as president of the Colonial Council in the first free election on American soil.

FIRST LEGISLATIVE ASSEMBLY IN AMERICA

The first legislative assembly in America, the House of Burgesses, met in the Episcopal church in Jamestown on July 30, 1619.

It was the beginning of representative government in the western continent.

Gov. George Yeardley had arrived at Jamestown from England in April 1619 with instructions from the London Company to bring about reform in the Virginia Colony. One of the instructions called for the establishment of a representative government, which would give the colonists virtually equal political status with the Company's General Assembly in London.

After some weeks of preparation, Yeardley issued a general proclamation setting in operation the Company's order. He proclaimed that there would be convened at the capital (Jamestown) on Friday, July 30, 1619, a General Assembly, "whereat were to be present the Governor and Counsell, with two burgesses from each plantation, freely to be elected by the inhabitantes thereof."

At that time, Virginia had about one thousand settlers living on eleven plantations. Elected to represent their plantation at the convening of the first General Assembly were:

For James City, Capt. William Powell, Ensign William Spence; for Charles City, Samuel Sharpe, Samuel Jordan; for the city of Henricus, Thomas Dowse, John Polentine; for Kicoatan, Capt. William Tucker, William Capps; for Capt. John Martin's plantation, Thomas Davis, Robert Stacy; for Smythe's Hundred, Capt. Thomas Graves, Walter Shelley; for Martin's Hundred, John Boys, John Jackson; for Argalls' Guifte, Mr. Pawlett, Edward Gourgaing; for Flower-dieu Hundred, Ensign Edmond Rosingham, John Jefferson; for Capt. Lawne's plantation, Capt. Christopher Lawne, Ensign Washer; for Capt. Ward's plantation, Capt. Ward, Lt. Gibbes.

The Counsel of Estate consisted of Capt. Samuel Macock, Capt. Nathaniel Powell, John Rolfe, Capt. Francis West and the Rev. William Wickham. In addition there were the speaker, John Pory; the minister; Rev. Richard Buck; the clerk, John Twine; the sergeant, Thomas Pierse.

Meeting in the Episcopal church in Jamestown, the twenty-two Burgesses were seated in the space ordinarily occupied by the congregation.

Each Burgess took the Oath of Supremacy, which ascertained that all holders of public office acknowledged the King of England not only as their civil sovereign but also as their spiritual leader. This alone was not enough to determine qualifications to be seated in the House of Burgesses. The House then considered the credentials of the elected members.

The Assembly refused to seat the Burgesses from Martin's Hundred, because the owner declined to give up certain previously granted privileges which rendered him almost independent of the government at Jamestown. So the number of Burgesses was reduced to twenty.

Jamestown was experiencing a heat wave when the first General Assembly men on Friday, July 30, 1619. On Wednesday, August 4, Gov. Yeardley resolved that the first session should end "by reason of extream heat, both paste and likely to ensue, and by that means of the alteration of the healthes of diverse of the general Assembly."

Several members became ill, and one Burgess, Walter Shelley, died on the third day of the Assembly because of the intense heat. Gov. Yeardley also felt the effects of the extreme heat.

Before the General Assembly ended its historic session, it had enacted twenty-eight statutes touching upon Indian affairs, the Church, land patents, the relations of servants and landlords, the planting of crops, the price of tobacco, foreign trade, and the general morality in Virginia.

The General Assembly claimed the exclusive right to levy general taxes. In the very first session it made use of this privilege by ordering, "That every man and manservant of above 16 years of age shall pay into the handes and Custody of the Burgesses of every Incorporation and plantation one pound of the best Tobacco." The funds thus raised were used for the payment of the officers of the Assembly.

The General Assembly was not only a legislative body, it was also a court of justice, and for many years served as the highest tribunal of the Virginia Colony.

The first General Assembly heard and passed on two judicial cases. One involved a servant having used bad words against his master and improper conduct with a maid. The "trecherous servante" was sentenced to have his ears nailed to a pilory for four days and to be publicly whipped each day.

The other case concerned a settler charged with speaking disrespectfully of the governor to Indian chief Opechanico. The man confessed and was censured, relieved of his militia rank, and condemned to serve the governor for seven years as an interpreter to the Indians.

The Burgesses who held that momentous meeting at Jamestown in 1619 began a political process that was the precursor of republican form government in America. Today the General Assembly of Virginia is the oldest continuous representative body in history among English-speaking peoples.

FIRST PROTEST AGAINST TAXATION WITHOUT REPRESENTATION

When the British Parliament in 1765 passed the Stamp Act to extract revenues from the colonists to finance the British army quartered in America, the reaction among the American colonies was quick and defiant: No taxation without representation. And Patrick Henry, a young lawyer from the Piedmont, gained everlasting fame when he stood up in the Virginia General Assembly to denounce King George III and to introduce resolutions opposing the Stamp Act.

While Patrick Henry and Virginians of his time have been credited for being the first to publicly oppose their government for imposing taxes without proper representation by the people, the first recorded protest against taxation without representation actually took place more than one hundred years earlier on the Eastern Shore of Virginia.

On March 30, 1651, the citizens of Northampton County presented a statement of grievances to the Virginia General Assembly protesting the unfairness of a tax imposed upon the county at a time when the county was not represented in the Legislature.

"Wee," they protested, "the Inhabitants of Northampton Countie doe complayne that from tyme to tyme (pticular yeares past) wee have been submitted & bine obedient unto the paymt of publeq Taxacons. Butt after the yeare 1647, since that tyme wee Conceive & have found that the taxes were very weightie. But in a more especiall manner (undr favor) wee are very sensible of the Taxacon of fforty sixe pounds of tobacco p. poll (this present yeare). And desire that the same bee taken off the charge of the Countie; furthermore wee alledge that after 1647, wee did understand & suppose our Countie of Northampton to bee disioynted & sequestered from the rest of Virginia. Therefore that Llawe wch requireth & inioyenth Taxacons from us to be Arbitrarye & illegall; forasmuch as wee had neither summons for Ellecon of Burgesses nor voyce in their Assemblie (during the time aforesd) but only the Singlur Burgess in September, Ano., 1651. Wee conceive that wee may Lawfullie ptest agt the pceedings in the Act of Assemblie for public Taxacons wch have relacon to Northmton Countie since the year 1647."

Northampton County's request that it be exempt from taxes due before it had a representative in the House of Burgesses went unheard. The General Assembly took no action on the protest.

While the Northampton tax protest was only a local affair, it enunciated the principle held among Virginia colonists that taxation without representation is unjust and illegal. This was one of the principles ultimately involved in the American Revolution.

FIRST AMONG PRESIDENTS

The image of George Washington, America's first president, and Martha Washington, the nation's first "first lady," are superimposed upon a letter Washington wrote to his wife in 1775. In the letter, Washington professed to Martha his "unalterable affection, which neither time or distance can change." Courtesy of the Virginia Division of Tourism

Virginia is known as "the mother of Presidents." Eight presidents of the United States were born in Virginia and that is more than were born in any other state.

The Virginia-born presidents were:

George Washington, the first President of the United States, was born February 22, 1732, the son of Augustine and Mary Ball Washington, at Wakefield on Pope's Creek, near Fredericksburg, Westmoreland County.

Actually, George Washington was born on February 11, based upon the Julian calendar then in use throughout the world. In 1582, Pope Gregory the Thirteenth ordained that ten days should be added to the tally of all past time since the birth of Jesus, to make up some fractional deficiencies in the calendar. The British government did not impose the calendar change on all its possessions, including the American colonies, until 1752. The British decreed that the day following September 2, 1752, should be called September 14, a loss of 11 days. All dates preceding were marked O. S. for Old Style. George Washington was born February 11, 1732, O. S., and after 1752 his birthday fell on February 22.

Washington was elected the first President of the United States of America and inaugurated on April 30, 1789. He was reelected in 1792, but refused to consider a third term, and retired to Mount Vernon on March 3, 1797.

Thomas Jefferson, the third President, was born April 13, 1743 (April 2, O. S.) at Shadwell, Goochland (now Albemarle) County. His parents were Peter and Jane Randolph Jefferson.

President Jefferson served two terms, from March 4, 1801 to March 3, 1809.

James Madison, the fourth President, was born March 16, 1751, (March 5, O. S.) at Port Conway, King George County. His parents were James and Eleanor Rose Conway Madison.

Madison was a two-term president, serving from March 4, 1809 to March 3, 1817.

James Monroe, the son of Spence and Elizabeth Monroe, was born April 28, 1758, in Westmoreland County. The fifth President of the United States, Monroe served two terms from March 4, 1817 to March 3, 1825.

The ninth President of the U.S., William Henry Harrison, was born February 9, 1773, at Berkeley, Charles City County. His parents were Benjamin and Elizabeth Bassett Harrison.

Harrison took office on March 4, 1841, but died a month later, on April 4, having caught pneumonia during the inauguration. He was the first U.S. president to die in office.

John Tyler, the tenth President, was born March 29, 1790, in Greenway, Charles City County. His parents were John and Mary Armistead Tyler.

Tyler took office as President on April 6, 1841, following the death of William Henry Harrison, and served until March 3, 1845.

Our twelfth president, Zachary Taylor, son of Richard and Sarah

Stother Taylor, was born November 24, 1784, at Montebello, Orange County.

He was sworn in as President on March 5, 1845, and died in office on July 9, 1850.

Woodrow Wilson, the twenty-eighth President, was born December 28, 1856, in Staunton. He was named Thomas Woodrow Wilson by his parents, Joseph Ruggles and Janet (Jessie) Wilson.

Woodrow Wilson served two terms as President, from March 4, 1913, to March 3, 1921.

FIRST CITY MANAGER

Charles E. Ashburner of Richmond became the first city manager in the United States on April 2, 1908, when the City Council elected him as the first general manager of Staunton.

Staunton, located in the heart of the historic Shenandoah Valley, was first settled in 1732. The hamlet was named in honor of Lady Staunton, the wife of Sir William Gooch who served as lieutenant governor of Virginia from 1727 to 1749.

By 1905, Staunton, then a conservative, prosperous city with a population of nearly 11,400, was administered by a city government consisting of a mayor and unicameral council of twelve members. The primary responsibility for administering the various municipal activities was vested in the council committees. However, the lack of cooperation between councilmen and the committees resulted in poor municipal management and high indebtedness. The ineptness of the city administration had brought about a wretched condition of city streets, most of them becoming a sea of mud whenever it rained.

Having passed the 10,000 population mark, Staunton in 1906 was required to establish a bicameral council consisting of a board of aldermen and a common council. But the new bicameral system was unwieldy and failed to produce any improvement in Staunton's governmental operations.

Alarmed over the doldrum and mismanagement of its city government, several leading Staunton citizens, led by John Crosby and Hugh G. Braxton, members of the Common Council, and W. O. Snydor, an alderman, in the summer of 1906 initiated a movement that called for Staunton to hire a general manager to run the city's day-to-day business.

Their movement came to fruition in January 1908 when the Common Council and the Board of Aldermen approved an ordinance creating the position of a general manager to take over from the council committees the direction of the city's administrative affairs.

The City Council, on April 2, 1908, elected Charles E. Ashburner as the first general manager of Staunton at an annual salary of $2,500. While the unofficial title of general manager was to be retained for many years, everyone in Staunton quickly settled on the use of "city manager" in the language of the day.

Charles Ashburner, the son of a British army officer, was born in Bombay, India, in 1870. He was educated in England, France, and Germany, and received his engineering degree from the University of Heidelberg. Before becoming city manager, he had been the maintenance engineer for the Staunton division of the Chesapeake and Ohio Railroad.

Ashburner was an aggressive person, and the vigor with which he tackled his job early won the plaudits of the community. Ashburner quickly got the city new paved streets, sewers, and bridges, and eliminated waste in purchasing of supplies for city departments.

Ashburner remained as a manager in Staunton until July 1911. Subsequently he became city manager of Springfield, Ohio; Norfolk, Virginia; and Stockton, California. He died in 1932.

Charles E. Ashburner was America's first city manager. He was elected by the Staunton City Council to manage the city's administrative affairs on April 2, 1908. Courtesy of the City of Staunton

113

FIRST ELECTED BLACK U.S. GOVERNOR

Lawrence Douglas Wilder, the grandson of slaves, became the first black elected U.S. governor when voters gave him a narrow victory over J. Marshall Coleman in the Virginia gubernatorial election on November 7, 1989.

Coleman contested the result, but Democrat Wilder's historic election was confirmed by the first statewide recount in Virginia. The recount of nearly 1.8 million votes declared Wilder the winner by 6,741 votes.

Wilder's victorious running mates were Donald S. Beyer, Jr., who was elected lieutenant governor, and Mary Sue Terry, who won re-election as state attorney general. In the 1985 election, Wilder was elected Virginia's first black lieutenant governor. In 1969, he became the first black elected to the Virginia State Senate since Reconstruction. Wilder was sworn in as governor on January 13, 1990.

Although Wilder became the nation's first elected black governor, another black, Pinckney B. S. Pinchback, served as the acting governor of Louisiana for thirty-four days in 1872-1873, after the elected governor was impeached in a bribery scandal.

Governor Wilder was born in Richmond on January 17, 1931.

A graduate of Virginia Union University, he received his law degree from Howard University in 1959. A Korean War veteran, Wilder won the Bronze Star when he and other soldiers captured twenty enemy troops on Pork Chop Hill.

L. Douglas Wilder, the nation's first elected black governor. Courtesy of the Office of the Governor, Richmond

INDUSTRY

FIRST GLASS FURNACE

The Jamestown settlers set up a glass furnace and started America's first industry—glassmaking—in 1608 on the shore of the James River a mile from Jamestown.

Because the London backers of the Jamestown settlement sought a financial return from their investment, workmen were sent to Virginia to produce glass, pitch, soap ash, and other salable items.

When the second supply ship reached Jamestown in October 1608, it brought along eight Dutch and Polish workmen, some who were skilled in making glass. They established their new industry a mile away from Jamestown, and began making glass from the coarse river sand.

When Capt. Christopher Newport sailed for England a few weeks later he carried with him "tryals of pitch, tarre, glasse, frankincense, sope ashes; with that clapboard and waynscot that could be provided." It is not known what kinds of glass were taken to England by Newport. Capt. John Smith, writing of the year 1609, stated: "...we made three or foure lotts of tarre, pitch, and sope ashes; produced a tryal of glass..." Again, the records do not reveal what kinds of glass were produced.

The original glassmaking effort was not successful. Nor did a second attempt work when a group of skilled Italian glass workers were brought to Jamestown in 1621 by Capt. William Norton. During the next three years, attempts were made to manufacture glass, but the Italian glassmakers complained that the "sand would not run," and it appears that only small amounts of glass were blown.

In 1931, the remains of the 1608 glass furnace were found and preserved, and a glasshouse was later reconstructed at Jamestown.

Archeologists have found fragments, pieces of window panes, small bottles and vials, and drinking glasses, from the early Jamestown glassmaking industry.

America's first industry—glassmaking—was established in 1608 when eight Dutch and Polish workers set up a glass furnace on the shore of the James River a mile from Jamestown. Here, at a reconstructed glasshouse in Jamestown, a costumed craftsman trained in seventeenth century glassblowing techniques, makes simple glass objects typical of those made in the early 1600s. Courtesy of the Virginia Division of Tourism

LABOR

FIRST BLACKS IN NORTH AMERICA

The first blacks to enter Virginia were landed in Jamestown from a Dutch privateer in late August 1619. Although a few blacks had accompanied Spanish explorers to the New World, these were the first of their race to arrive in English North America.

The twenty blacks, of whom at least three were women, were promptly sold to the settlers as servants. The first blacks were not considered to be slaves, but indentured servants.

Most of the hard labor at the Jamestown settlement was done by English indentured servants—men and women who had agreed to work for a fixed period of years to pay their passage.

Another reason why the first blacks at Jamestown were not slaves was the fact that they had been baptized, and by English law, which then governed Virginia, a slave who had been converted to Christianity became "enfranchised." However, in 1667, the Virginia General Assembly passed a law declaring that baptism does not bring freedom.

While the first twenty blacks in Virginia started their life in Jamestown as indentured servants, their status in society was tantamount to being slaves. Historical documents from the early Jamestown era showed that in many instances it was considered customary practice to hold some blacks in a form of life service.

As the British colonists increased their agricultural production, especially that of tobacco, they found that slavery had marked advantages over servitude. The slave's service was for life, whereas the indentured servant only worked for a time. By 1661, slavery was recognized in the statutory law of the Virginia Colony.

FIRST CCC CAMP

Camp Roosevelt, the nation's first Civilian Conservation Corps camp, opened in the George Washington National Forest near Luray on April 17, 1933.

The Civilian Conservation Corps (CCC) was initiated by Pres. Franklin D. Roosevelt during the Great Depression to save both human and natural resources by putting unemployed young men to work in American forests.

The CCC was authorized by the U.S. Congress on March 31, 1933, and the first enrollments began on April 5, when Robert Fechner, vice president of the Machinists' Union, was appointed director of the CCC.

The Labor Department, War Department (Army) and the Forestry Service set up the CCC organization. The Army supplied and managed the camps, and provided equipment and transportation.

Within two months, the CCC enrolled 250,000 young men from relief families in some 1,500 camps where they were put to the useful work of reforestation, flood control, and soil conservation. The young men enrolled for a six-month stint. They received a dollar a day, but a portion of their pay was sent home to their families.

By 1935, the CCC had reached a maximum strength of 500,000; by 1942, when the project ended, more than 2,250,000 youths had served in the undertaking.

In Virginia, five thousand young men enrolled when the Civilian Conservation Corps was first started. By the end of the program, more than 107,000 Virginians had been employed by the CCC in more than eighty camps (twelve of them for blacks).

Virginia CCC enrollees planted 15.2 million trees, built 986 bridges, reduced fire hazards in 152,000 acres of forest, and helped develop Virginia's state park system. They also stocked rivers and streams with fish, strung over two thousand miles of telephone lines, and participated in the restoration of historic sites.

MARITIME

FIRST STEAMBOAT

James Fulton is generally recognized as the man who built the first commercially successful steamboat, but on December 3, 1787, twenty years before Fulton's success, James Rumsey successfully demonstrated the world's first steamboat on the waters of the Potomac River at Shepherdstown, Virginia (now West Virginia).

A large crowd had gathered at Shepherdstown to witness Rumsey demonstrate his latest invention. Gen. Horatio Gates, a major general in the Continental Army, and other prominent citizens of the neighborhood were present.

When the boat was ready, Rumsey would not permit anyone except himself, Capt. Charles Morrow, and several ladies to go aboard for the first experimental trip.

The boat was propelled by streams of water forced out through the stern by a force pump operated by a steam engine. To the cheers of onlookers, the boat was driven upstream against the current at the speed of three miles an hour. The boat steamed up and down the river for two hours before returning to the dock.

Gen. Gates was quite excited about James Rumsey's steamboat. In a statement commenting upon the steamboat experiment, Gates anticipated the future when he wrote, "I have not the least doubt but it may be brought into common and beneficial use, and be of advantage to all navigation..."

Rumsey made a second and even more successful trial of his boat on December 14, 1787, this time loading the boat with more weight. Even with the added burden, the boat attained a speed of four miles an hour—an amazing speed at that time.

James Rumsey was a native of Maryland and had been a soldier in the American Revolution. At the close of the war he located at Bath, Virginia, now Berkeley Springs, West Virginia. An ingenious mechanic who taught himself to apply scientific principles to his work, Rumsey began working on mills, modifying their wheels and machines. He received numerous state patents before establishment of the federal patent system.

Before he invented the steamboat, James Rumsey had developed and received a patent for a mechanical pole boat for moving a boat upstream. Rumsey demonstrated the boat for George Washington at Bath in September 1784, and Washington issued a certificate supporting Rumsey's invention. While nothing became of the pole boat, its development eventually led Rumsey to invent the steamboat.

Having successfully demonstrated the practicability of steam navigation, James Rumsey went to Philadelphia to present his ideas for inventions to the American Philosophical Society. Led by Benjamin Franklin, members of the Society formed the Rumseian Society to raise money to send Rumsey to England to exploit his invention.

James Rumsey met with considerable success in England. He developed an improved steamboat but just before it was to be tested on the Thames River, Rumsey died December 20, 1792, of an apoplectic stroke while delivering a lecture on his inventions.

James Rumsey, inventor and mechanic, successfully demonstrated the world's first steamboat on the Potomac River at Shepherdstown, Virginia (now West Virginia) on December 3, 1787. This portrait of Rumsey was painted by British artist Benjamin West. Courtesy of Frederick T. Newbraugh

125

The old Cape Henry Lighthouse at Virginia Beach is the first lighthouse authorized by the first U.S. Congress. It lighted the entrance to the Chesapeake Bay from 1792 to 1881. Courtesy of the City of Virginia Beach, Office of Public Information

OLD CAPE HENRY LIGHTHOUSE

FIRST LIGHTHOUSE AUTHORIZED BY THE FIRST UNITED STATES CONGRESS. ERECTED IN 1791. IT LIGHTED THE ENTRANCE INTO CHESAPEAKE BAY UNTIL 1881. IT IS MAINTAINED BY THE CITY OF VIRGINIA BEACH AND IS THE OFFICIAL SYMBOL OF THE CITY.

OWNED BY THE ASSOCIATION
FOR THE PRESERVATION OF
VIRGINIA ANTIQUITIES

Two of the nation's historic lighthouses are located at Cape Henry, Virginia. In front, distinguished by its black and white vertical stripes, is the nation's first cast iron lighthouse. In the rear is the old Cape Henry Lighthouse. Courtesy of the Fifth Coast Guard District

FIRST LIGHTHOUSE

Upon the highest sand hill at Cape Henry stands the first lighthouse and the first building authorized in the first session of the first United States Congress in 1789. The first Congress provided for the "establishment and support of light houses, beacons, buoys, and public piers." The act transferred the twelve lighthouses then in existence from the jurisdiction of the states to the federal government, and ordered "that a light house shall be erected near the entrance to the Chesapeake Bay."

Congressional signers of the act which created the Cape Henry Lighthouse, the first lighthouse to be built by the federal government, was Frederick Augustus Muhlenberg, Speaker of the House, and John Adams, President of the Senate. The legislation was approved August 7, 1789, by Pres. George Washington.

Ever since the first permanent English settlers landed at Cape Henry in 1607, the colonists had been aware of the need of a navigational beacon to aid mariners entering the Chesapeake Bay. In 1720, Gov. Alexander Spotswood called upon the House of Burgesses to build and keep a lighthouse at Cape Henry and to seek out the assistance of Maryland to construct and maintain the lighthouse. Nothing became of Gov. Spotswood's request. For many years thereafter, Virginia and Maryland officials discussed the matter of a lighthouse at Cape Henry to no avail.

Pres. Washington took a special interest in the Cape Henry Lighthouse project after his former aide-de-camp during the Revolution, Gov. Edmund Randolph, wrote the president for support. Randolph offered to sell stones for the construction of the lighthouse and to cede two acres of land at Cape Henry to the U.S. government.

The first congressional appropriation for lighthouses became law on March 26, 1790. The amount was $24,076.66.

On March 31, 1791, the federal government awarded a contract to John McComb, Jr., a bricklayer from New York, to build the Cape Henry Lighthouse at the cost of $17,500. The ninety-foot tall lighthouse, an octagonal sandstone tower, was completed in 1792. A local man, Laban Gossigan, became the first keeper.

The light, which became operative in October 1792, first consisted of oil lamps burning in turn fish oil, sperm oil, colza oil, lard oil, and finally kerosene after the discovery of petroleum in Pennsylvania in 1859. A fog bell was added in 1855. In 1857, the lighthouse was provided with a dioptric Fresnel lens, making the light visible for twenty-four miles.

During the Civil War, in April 1861, the Princess Anne County Militia attacked the lighthouse and destroyed the lens. When the light was placed back in operation in 1863, it was guarded by federal troops from Fort Monroe.

By 1872, cracks appeared in the walls of the tower, and the Lighthouse Board recommended the building of a new tower because the old Cape Henry Lighthouse "is in danger of being thrown down by some heavy gale."

A new cast iron lighthouse was constructed and its first light was shown in December 1881.

The old Cape Henry Lighthouse remained standing, and in 1930 it was acquired from the U.S. government by the Association for the Preservation of Virginia Antiquities. By 1934, the lighthouse was restored and made safe for visitors. In 1964, the lighthouse became recognized as a Registered National Historic Landmark.

In 1970, the Association for the Preservation of Virginia Antiquities leased the lighthouse to the city of Virginia Beach for $1.00 per year. The old Cape Henry Lighthouse is open to visitors Memorial Day through Labor Day.

FIRST CAST IRON LIGHTHOUSE

When the stone-towered Cape Henry Lighthouse, the first lighthouse to be built by the U.S. government, was declared unsafe and "in danger of being thrown down by some heavy gale," the Lighthouse Board in 1872 recommended it be replaced by a new structure—the first cast iron lighthouse in the nation.

It was not until 1875 that Congress appropriated $75,000 to build a new lighthouse at Cape Henry. In 1879, a contract for a new iron lighthouse, consisting of cast-iron plates bolted into masonry walls, was entered into with Morris Tasker & Company of Philadelphia. Congress voted two more appropriations of twenty-five thousand dollars each in 1880 and 1881.

Building the new cast iron lighthouse was not without problems. The construction company erected a temporary pier at Cape Henry in August 1880 in order to land equipment and supplies for the lighthouse. The first freight car onto the pier plunged off into the Chesapeake Bay and the entire pier collapsed just after contractors had salvaged their supplies. A seven mile railroad spur was then built

to haul supplies overland from Lynnhaven Inlet to the
construction site.

The nation's first cast iron lighthouse was completed in
November 1881. Cast-iron plates of the 170-foot high structure were
painted in alternating vertical stripes of black and white for easy
identification by mariners.

The new Cape Henry Lighthouse was first lit on December 15,
1881. It was equipped with a Fresnel lense of polished glass made in
Paris, France. With modifications in the light sources from an oil wick
to a 160,000 candlepower electric light, the lense is still in use.

In December 1983, the cast iron lighthouse at Cape Henry became
the last lighthouse in Virginia to be manned by a lighthouse keeper
and crew. The lighthouse became automated, controlled electronically
from the Coast Guard Support Center near Craney Island
in Portsmouth.

FIRST LIGHTSHIP

The first lightship in the United States was stationed off
Willoughby Spit, the entrance to Hampton Roads, in the summer
of 1820.

The first lightship was authorized in 1819 when Congress
appropriated funds for the first of two vessels to be used in the lower
Chesapeake Bay. In September 1819, a contract was awarded to John
Pool of Hampton for the construction of a vessel –"a floating light" –of
seventy tons, with "two square lanterns three feet wide and five feet
high." The lanterns, hung from the ship's mast, contained from ten to
twelve wicks. The lightship had two anchors to keep it in a
steady position.

The choppy waters off Willoughby Spit were too rough for the
small lightship, so within a few months it was moved to a more
protective location near Craney Island.

Despite the unseaworthiness of the first lightship, favorable
reports from mariners who realized the value of lightships stationed at
strategic locations, caused the government to construct four larger
lightships for placement at various locations on the Chesapeake Bay.

MARRIAGE

FIRST WHITE MARRIAGE IN AMERICA

The first marriage of a white couple in America took place at Jamestown in December 1608 between Anne Burras and John Laydon.

John Laydon, a carpenter, was one of twelve laborers who settled at Jamestown in May 1607. He had arrived from England aboard the *Susan Constant*, one of the three ships which brought English settlers to Virginia under auspices of the London Company.

Anne Burras, maid to Mistress Forrest, wife of Thomas Forrest, arrived at Jamestown in October 1608 aboard the supply ship, *Mary and Margaret*. They were the first women to arrive in the Jamestown Colony.

Since being the only single woman at the Jamestown Colony, Miss Burras no doubt was sought out by many men, but John Laydon was the successful suitor. They were married around Christmas 1608 in a church that had been rebuilt after a fire that destroyed most of the Jamestown settlement in January of that year.

The Burras-Laydon marriage was the first wedding of English people in America. John was thirty-eight, while Anne was only fourteen years old. Their marriage produced four children, all girls. Their first daughter, named Virginia, born in 1609, was the first white child to be born in Virginia. The other Laydon children were Alice, Katherine, and Margaret.

Virginia Laydon was not the first white child born in America. That honor belongs to Virginia Dare, born in 1587 at Roanoke Island, then in Virginia, but now North Carolina. Her parents were Ananias and Eleanor Dare. The Dares were members of the unfortunate "Lost Colony" settlers who vanished without a trace.

FIRST MIXED MARRIAGE

The first marriage between persons of different races in America took place on April 5, 1614, when John Rolfe, a British colonist, and Pocahontas, an Indian princess, were married in the Episcopal church at Jamestown, with Parson Richard Buck officiating.

Pocahontas, then about seventeen or eighteen years old, was the favorite daughter of the Algonquin Indian chief Powhatan. Her first appearance in recorded history was on the occasion of her saving the life of John Smith, a leader of the Jamestown settlement. In December 1607, Capt. Smith, on an exploration trip up the Chickahominy River, was captured by Indians. After several weeks in captivity, Smith was led to a large stone and made to lay down his head. Powhatan ordered his men to beat out Smith's brains with clubs. As the warriors raised their clubs to strike Smith, Pocahontas rushed forward, put his head in her arms, and begged her father to spare his life. Powhatan agreed, and let Smith return safely to Jamestown.

While historians at times doubted the authenticity of John Smith's account of the Pocahontas incident, the story gained credibility as we learned more about Indian life. In Indian warfare women, children, chiefs, and sometimes outstanding male warriors were spared. Male warriors, who showed great courage and strength were often adopted into the victor's tribe following a ritual of mock execution. Smith may not have understood that the mock execution ritual was in reality an Indian adoption ceremony for a warrior.

In the spring of 1613, Capt. Samuel Argall sailed his ship up the Potomac River to trade with Indians. Learning that Pocahontas was in the area, he induced the local Indian chief to lure her aboard the ship. Returning to Jamestown with Pocahontas as a hostage, Argall turned her over to the governor of Jamestown, Sir Thomas Gates, who treated her as a guest rather than as a prisoner.

Gates placed Pocahontas under the care of Sir Thomas Dale, Marshal of Virginia, who in turn entrusted her to Rev. Alexander Whitaker, the minister of Henrico, a new settlement. Whitaker taught Pocahontas English, instructed her in Christianity, and baptized her Rebecca. Her Indian name was actually Matoaka; Pocahontas was a nickname which meant "playful one" or "frolicsome."

It was during her stay at Henrico that Pocahontas met John Rolfe, a widower who had been shipwrecked at Bermuda before arriving at Jamestown in 1610. Then about twenty-eight years old, Rolfe was an industrious man who was the first of the Jamestown colonists to cultivate tobacco for export to England.

Rolfe fell in love with the young Indian girl and wrote Dale a lengthy letter setting forth the many reasons why he should be given permission to marry this "unbelieving creature." Sir Dale, seeing the good that could come out of the marriage of Powhatan's daughter and a leading colonist, agreed to the marriage. Powhatan agreed, too, and the marriage brought several years of peace between the Indians and the Jamestown colonists.

In May 1616, Rolfe and Pocahontas and their one-year old son Thomas left Jamestown for England. Pocahontas was honored as a princess by the London society, and was eventually presented to King James I and Queen Anne.

In early 1617, Rolfe and his family prepared to return to Jamestown. Before their vessel had cleared the port of Gravesend, Pocahontas fell ill, probably from pneumonia, and died. She was buried in the parish church of St. George at Gravesend on March 21, 1617.

Rolfe later returned to Jamestown, but his son remained in England with relatives. Rolfe was probably killed in the great Indian massacre of 1622. His son Thomas came to America about 1640 and married a Virginia girl named Jane Poythress. Many Virginia families proudly trace their descent from this union and direct linkage to the Indian princess Pocahontas.

FIRST WOMAN TO REFUSE TO SUBMIT TO THE "OBEY" IN THE MARRIAGE VOW

Latter day women's liberationists will proudly hail Sarah Harrison of Surry County as a champion of women's rights. She was the first American woman to refuse to accede to the "obey" in the marriage ceremony.

It happened in colonial Virginia.

Men outnumbered women in those times, but this unbalance in sex ratio often resulted in a woman being in a favorable bargaining position when she entered into marriage.

This was the case of Sarah Harrison, a handsome and strong-willed lady of the influential Harrison family that would produce a Virginia governor and two American presidents.

In 1687, Sarah Harrison agreed to marry Dr. James Blair, founder of the College of William and Mary in Williamsburg. Under Virginia and Anglican church laws, the wife had to submit to the husband's authority as soon as she said "I do."

Sarah Harrison, however, had other ideas.

At her wedding ceremony, when the Rev. Smith, reading from the Prayer Book, reached the line, "Will thou love him, comfort him, honor and obey...," Sarah interrupted with a loud, "No obey!"

After a moment of embarrassing silence, the minister repeated the question.

"No obey!," said Sarah again.

The Rev. Smith tried once again. "No obey!," said Sarah, for the third time.

The minister, having gotten Sarah's message, continued uninterrupted with the rest of the wedding ceremony.

Stubborn Sarah Harrison, having made her point, in the end answered that "I will," and became the wife of Dr. Blair.

FIRST WEDDING IN A BOXING RING

The first wedding in a boxing ring took place at the Pavilion Convention Center in Virginia Beach on December 21, 1985, when professional lightweight boxer Pernell "Sweetpea" Whitaker married Rovonda Anthony. Both bride and bridegroom were from Norfolk.

Whitaker was originally scheduled to box at the fight card held at the Pavilion Convention Center, but broke his left foot two weeks earlier. Lou Duva, Whitaker's manager, concocted the idea of having his popular fighter be married in the ring, following the scheduled fights.

The wedding ceremony was performed by Rev. I. Joseph Williams of the Antioch Church in Norfolk. When the wedding was complete, and the couple had been pronounced husband and wife, Sweetpea Whitaker grabbed Rovonda's hand and lifted it triumphantly into the air as a ring announcer would declare a boxer the winner of a fight.

Pernell Whitaker won the Olympic gold medal for boxing in the 132-pound class during the 1984 Summer Olympic Games held in Los Angeles. He captured the Olympic title by scoring a knock out victory over Luis Ortiz of Puerto Rico. As an amateur boxer, Whitaker also won gold medals in the 132-pound class during the 1982 Pan American Games and the 1983 World Championships. His overall amateur record was 201-14 with 92 KO's.

Whitaker turned professional after the 1984 Olympic Games. In 1989, Whitaker won the International Boxing Federation World lightweight title by defeating Greg Haugen in twelve rounds.

Shown here is the first wedding ceremony to take place in a boxing ring. Professional lightweight boxer Pernell "Sweetpea" Whitaker and Rovonda Anthony took their vows in the ring at the Pavilion Convention Center in Virginia Beach on December 21, 1985. Courtesy of Lois Bernstein

Boxer Pernell "Sweet-pea" Whitaker lifts the arm of his bride Rovonda Anthony in a victorious fighter's pose after they became the first couple to be wed in a boxing ring. Courtesy of Lois Bernstein

MEDICAL

This depicts the statue of Capt. John Smith at Jamestown Island. Capt. Smith, soldier, adventurer, one of the first settlers at Jamestown and once governor of Virginia, was saved from execution by Indian princess Pocahontas. Dr. Walter Russell, the first physician in America, saved Smith's life when the explorer was poisoned by a stingray he had speared near the mouth of the Rappahannock River. Courtesy of the Virginia Division of Tourism

FIRST PHYSICIAN

Dr. Walter Russell, the first physician in America, arrived at Jamestown in January 1608 when Capt. Christopher Newport returned from England with a shipment of food and equipment to supply the first permanent settlers in the New World.

The Jamestown settlers had undergone a period of hard times, with low provisions, and an epidemic of diseases which had killed many people.

While no doubt Dr. Russell did his best to aid the suffering settlers, history does not record the medical treatments he rendered during the time of great need. But Dr. Russell's services to the heroic Capt. John Smith, a leader of the Jamestown Colony, is recorded for posterity.

In the summer of 1608, Capt. Smith led a party of twelve to explore the headwaters of the Chesapeake Bay. Near the mouth of the Rappahannock River, Smith speared a stingray, but the fish took revenge by wounding Smith with its barbed and poisonous tail.

Smith became so ill that it was feared he would die. Four hours after the accident, Smith is said to have ordered his companions to prepare his grave.

But Dr. Russell, a member of the exploring party, probed the wound, and applied a "precious oile," which eased the captain's pain so well that he ate the fish for his supper.

The place where Dr. Russell saved Captain Smith's life is now called Stingray Point.

FIRST MENTAL HOSPITAL

America's first public institution devoted exclusively to the care and treatment of the mentally ill opened its doors on October 12, 1773, as the "Public Hospital for Persons of Insane and Disordered Minds" in Williamsburg. The first patients were two insane persons who had been taken from the jail in Williamsburg. They had been held in jail only because there had been no other public place to keep insane persons.

Until the hospital was built, mentally ill persons in Virginia were given little or no help. Some were assisted by family and friends; insane paupers were sometimes cared for by the local community. But by and large, the mentally ill were neglected and left to wander about, often abused by indifferent fellow citizens. Those considered violent and dangerous were confined in jail or in privately-built log cages.

In 1766, Virginia's royal governor, Francis Fauquier, expressed sympathy for the mentally ill when he warned the House of Burgesses of "a poor unhappy set of people who are deprived of their senses and wander about the country side terrifying the rest of their fellow creatures."

Fauquier appealed to the legislators for their "consideration and humanity." He asked that the Colonial legislature establish a public hospital to help the mentally ill.

Not until 1770 did the Virginia General Assembly act upon Fauquier's request. The legislators enacted a law providing "for the Support and Maintenance of Ideots, Lunatics, and other Persons of unsound mind."

The two-story brick hospital, built on the southern edge of Williamsburg, was completed in 1773. It contained twenty-four cells for patients, but only twelve patients "of lost reason" were moved into the hospital during its first year of operation.

The first keeper of the hospital was James Galt, former head of the public jail. His wife Mary became the first matron. Galt would call upon Dr. John de Sequeyra, the hospital's first consulting physician, for medical advice and assistance.

Treatments of the early patients consisted of crude methods then in use in British asylums. Patients were bled to reduce pressures on the "diseased" brain, and were often placed in chains, at the first sign of violence.

Over the years the hospital grew to a complex of eleven buildings housing 450 patients, and became known as the Eastern State Hospital. The original building burned in the night of June 7, 1885. It has recently been reconstructed in Colonial Williamsburg as an exhibit of the nation's first public institution devoted to the mentally ill.

FIRST MARINE HOSPITAL

The first Marine Hospital in America was located in the town of Washington, now Berkley in Norfolk. It was established by an act passed on December 20, 1787, by the Virginia Legislature. The legislation authorized the purchase of land and the building of a hospital "for the reception of aged, sick and disabled seamen."

The building was erected by Robert Bolland, a resident of Portsmouth, whose father had formerly been a surgeon in the British Royal Navy.

The first move to create the hospital was begun in 1782, when the Virginia General Assembly enacted a law requiring the captain of every vessel entering port to pay a tax of one shilling per sailor aboard. The funds would be used to build a marine hospital.

Virginians had shown concern for the health and welfare of its sailors long before the first marine hospital was built. As early as 1708, the Council of Colonial Virginia ordered that a house be put to use for the sick seamen of the Royal Navy. In 1727, the General Assembly ordered that ship captains be punished if they put sick or disabled seamen ashore without providing for their care.

The Marine Hospital suffered from its beginning for lack of sufficient operating funds. In 1798, the Virginia Legislature voted to authorize the governor to sell the property to the United States government, which by then had taken steps to establish marine hospitals for the relief of sick and disabled seamen.

The deed of sale between the Commonwealth of Virginia and the United States government, dated April 20, 1801, was signed by Gov. James Monroe.

Virginia's first Marine Hospital thus became the first Marine Hospital acquired by the United States government. A second government marine hospital was acquired in Boston in 1802, but it was not until 1837 that a third marine hospital was built in New Orleans.

The hospitals were operated by the Marine Hospital Service, which was created by Congress in 1798. Initially, the Marine Hospital in Berkley was under the control of a U.S. Navy surgeon.

The Marine Hospital at Berkley continued to be used by both merchant and naval seamen until the Civil War. The Confederates then took over and used it for barracks. After the Confederates evacuated Norfolk the Federal troops took it over as an Army hospital and used it until 1862.

The war had ruined the commerce of Norfolk, and since Berkley was not accessible to the city as it is today, the military closed the Marine Hospital and sent patients to St. Vincent's Hospital in Norfolk, forerunner of DePaul Hospital.

In 1869, the government sold the Marine Hospital building to Albert T. Nichols for $15,600. Later it became the Ryland Institute. In 1904, it became the property of Paul Garrett, who used it as a residence adjacent to his wine manufacturing business in Berkley. Mr. Garrett later sold the property to the Imperial Tobacco Company.

Finally, in January 1933, the building was demolished to make way for the construction of the bridge-tunnel joining Norfolk, Portsmouth, and Berkley.

The nation's first Marine Hospital, located at Berkley in Norfolk, was established by the Virginia Legislature on December 20, 1787. Virginia was the first state in the nation to provide hospital services to aged, sick and disabled seamen. Courtesy of the Kirn Memorial Library, Norfolk

145

FIRST U.S. NAVAL HOSPITAL

On April 2, 1827, the cornerstone of the first U.S. Naval Hospital was laid in Portsmouth at the site of Fort Nelson. Built of granite and freestone, with architect John Haviland of Philadelphia in charge, the hospital was completed in 1834.

While Congress appropriated funds for the construction of the hospital, the U.S. Navy established a Hospital Fund to build the Naval Hospital in Portsmouth and a Naval Asylum at Philadelphia. Monies that were accumulated for the Hospital Fund were obtained by deducting twenty cents per month from the pay of naval personnel.

The need for the hospital forced its occupancy and use before it was completed. The north wing was selected as the most completed part of the building and placed in commission in July 1830. The entire staff was composed of surgeon Thomas Williamson, two attendants, two washers, and one cook.

The first patient was an officer who "suffered from partial aberration of mind, and requiring him to be subjected to a state of constant confinement and restraint."

During the early years of the Portsmouth Naval Hospital, one commanding officer practiced economy and attempted to make a twenty-five cents daily ration allotment cover all of the hospital's expenses for each patient.

Since its commissioning in 1830, the U.S. Naval Hospital in Portsmouth has occupied a prominent position in the lives of Navy personnel assigned to the Hampton Roads area. Expansion over the years was capped by the opening of a new, sixteen-story facility in June 1960.

The cornerstone of the first U.S. Naval Hospital in Portsmouth was laid on April 2, 1827. While the first patient was admitted in July 1830, the building was not completed until 1834. This photograph shows the Portsmouth Naval Hospital in 1875. Courtesy of the U.S. Navy

Construction for the first U.S. Naval Hospital (front) in Portsmouth began on April 2, 1827. A new sixteen-story hospital (background) was completed in June 1960. Courtesy of the U.S. Navy

FIRST HOSPITAL TO TREAT PATIENTS
BY PSYCHIC READINGS

The Cayce Hospital at Virginia Beach was the nation's first hospital to treat patients on the basis of psychic readings. The hospital, which first opened on November 11, 1928, treated patients in accordance with medical readings of psychic Edgar Cayce and under the supervision of a medical staff headed by Dr. Thomas B. House.

Edgar Cayce discovered his psychic ability as a young man. He found that he could enter a self-induced sleep and diagnose illnesses and prescribe treatments for people he had never seen. Subsequently he provided information, or "readings," on numerous subjects. The scope of his work included information and advice on thousands of subjects, including mental and spiritual counsel, metaphysics, parapsychology, religion, and prophecy of personal and world events.

The first patient admitted to the Cayce Hospital on November 12, 1928, was a man suffering from sinus irritation and whose blood showed diabetic tendencies. Cayce went into a hypnotic trance and his psychic reading suggested that the patient's treatment include baths, packs, osteopathy, medicine, and proper diet. Two weeks later the patient was released, well enough to return to work.

The hospital closed its doors on February 28, 1931, when its chief patron, Morton Blumenthal, a New York financier, withdrew his support after suffering heavy losses in the stock market crash of 1929.

The original hospital building now serves as headquarters for the Association for Research and Enlightenment, Inc., a non-profit organization which has preserved the work of Edgar Cayce.

FIRST MEDICAL SCHOOL BUILT BY PUBLIC CONTRIBUTIONS

Eastern Virginia Medical School in Norfolk, which opened its doors on September 28, 1973, with a three-year curriculum and twenty-four students, is the nation's first medical school to be built solely by public contributions. The school now serves as the focal point for training and placing health care professionals throughout the region.

One of the first moves toward establishing the medical school occurred in 1964 when the Virginia General Assembly created the Norfolk Area Medical Center Authority. The Legislature changed the name to the Eastern Virginia Medical Authority in 1975 as acknowledgment of its broad base throughout Hampton Roads.

Among the objectives of the Authority was the creation of a regional medical school. The Eastern Virginia Medical School was started with a $15 million fund drive initiated through the effort of community leaders led by retired U.S. congressman Porter Hardy, Jr. The EVMS continues to be privately financed. The Commonwealth of

Virginia and the seven cities of Hampton Roads (Norfolk, Portsmouth, Chesapeake, Suffolk, Virginia Beach, Newport News, and Hampton) provide partial funding for operating costs.

The proposal for the medical school did not include the building of a new hospital but rather the participation of existing community and federal health facilities in providing clinical instruction. While the first EVMS students received their basic medical training in Smith-Rogers Hall, their initial clinical training was obtained in the Children's Hospital of The King's Daughters, DePaul Hospital, Medical Center Hospitals, U.S. Naval Hospital, and the Veterans Administration Center.

Today EVMS is associated with twenty-nine hospitals and regional health care facilities. Basic medical training is given in Lewis Hall.

In 1973, Eastern Virginia Medical School moved its curriculum from three to four years. A graduate school of medicine was founded in 1975.

Some 340 students now comprise the EVMS student body. To teach them is a 167-member, full-time faculty with the additional resources of eight hundred community physicians, who are volunteer professors and instructors.

Lewis Hall is the basic medical education building of the Eastern Virginia Medical School. The building, named in honor of Sydney and Frances Lewis, was dedicated February 18, 1978. Courtesy of Eastern Virginia Medical Authority

149

Students leave after attending basic medical courses in Lewis Hall of the Eastern Virginia Medical School. EVMS, which opened its doors on September 28, 1973, is the nation's first medical school built solely by public funds. Courtesy of Eastern Virginia Medical Authority

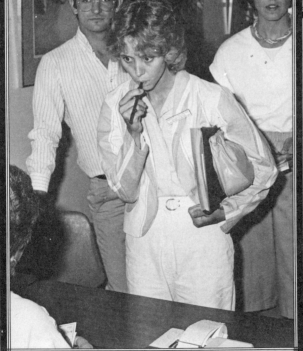

Students register to enter Eastern Virginia Medical School in Norfolk. Preference is given to Virginia students, especially current and former residents of Hampton Roads. Courtesy of Eastern Virginia Medical Authority

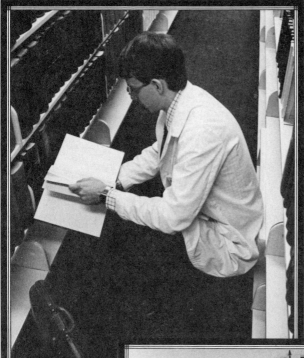

A large medical library is available to students at the Eastern Virginia Medical School in Norfolk. Courtesy of Eastern Virginia Medical Authority

A student at the Eastern Virginia Medical School observes a physician examining a child patient at a Hampton Roads health facility providing clinical instructions to EVMS students. Some eight hundred physicians in Hampton Roads are volunteer professors and instructors at EVMS. Courtesy of Eastern Virginia Medical Authority

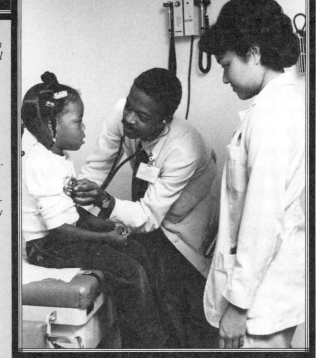

FIRST MOTHER-INFANT PROGRAM
TO CURB CHILD ABUSE

Portsmouth Psychiatric Center became the first psychiatric hospital in the world to begin a program to curb child abuse when it opened its Mother-Infant Unit on December 15, 1986. Courtesy of Portsmouth Psychiatric Center

Lynn C. Blackwood, Jr., Ph.D., is first director of the Mother-Infant Unit of Portsmouth Psychiatric Center. Courtesy of Portsmouth Psychiatric Center

Portsmouth Psychiatric Center on December 15, 1986, opened a new unit devoted exclusively to mothers and their infants. The unit, named the Mother-Infant Unit, was part of a new program designed to prevent and treat child abuse, neglect, and problems in the early relationship between parent and child that can lead to academic and social difficulties later in the child's life.

Portsmouth Psychiatric Center thus became the first psychiatric hospital in the world to treat both mothers and infants at the same time, allowing them to stay in the same room. The first mother and child patients were admitted to the Mother–Infant Unit on December 17, 1986.

Lynn C. Blackwood, Jr., Ph.D., director of the Mother–Infant Unit, called the Unit a forerunner in the trend toward preventive mental health.

"With early detection of disturbances in the parent–child relationship and intensive treatment efforts, we will hopefully prevent a serious attachment disturbance between the parent and child from occurring. By so doing, we protect the child and family from future social and academic failures and allow the child to reach his or her fullest potential. We also will be preventing the transfer of abusive patterns from this generation to the next, as we know abused children frequently go on to become abusive parents," Dr. Blackwood explained.

Mother and child patients spend about forty-five days at the Portsmouth Psychiatric Center. When mother and child leave the hospital, they continue to receive outpatient treatment.

FIRST AMONG HOSPITAL FIRSTS

Norfolk General Hospital is one of the nation's most innovative medical centers. It has an impressive record of medical firsts.

The 644-bed Norfolk General Hospital, a privately-owned, not-for-profit medical center, dates back to 1888 when the Women's Christian Association organized a 25-bed hospital which they called "Retreat For The Sick."

In 1898, the hospital moved to a new facility and became the Norfolk Protestant Hospital. In 1903, the expanded hospital was renamed again, this time, Norfolk General. The latest change of name took place in 1987—to Sentara Norfolk General Hospital.

Over the years, Norfolk General has emerged as a major medical center where physicians and researchers have made important contributions to medical science.

Here are some of the exciting medical first achieved at Norfolk General Hospital:

Charles E. Horton, MD, with Plastic Surgery Specialists Inc., in Norfolk, and Charles E. Devine, Jr., MD, with Devine-Fiveash Associates, Ltd., Norfolk, were the first surgeons in the world to do a one-stage repair of hypospadias (a urogenital deformity) in 1961.

Horton and Devine were also the first surgeons to sew the penis back on by connecting flesh with nerves, arteries and veins from a boy's abdomen. Their work enabled the boy to eventually lead a normal sex life. This surgery was first performed in 1982.

Dr. Horton was the first in the country to do immediate post masectomy reconstruction at the time of masectomy utilizing pectoral muscles. This surgery was performed in 1974.

John B. McCraw, MD, FACS with Plastic Surgery Specialists Inc., Norfolk, was the first surgeon in the world to use myocutaneous flaps in reconstructive surgery at Norfolk General Hospital in 1972. This revolutionary procedure involves replacing injured or disease damaged tissue with healthy tissue. It enables surgeons to reconstruct parts of the body that are severely disfigured by surgery or disease.

Dr. McCraw was the first in the nation to perfect silicone gel implants to enlarge women's breasts. His work in breast reconstruction was performed at Norfolk General in 1977. McCraw has also pioneered techniques involving the latissimus dorsi myocutaneous muscle and the rectus abdominous muscle for breast reconstruction.

Jerry O. Penix, MD, of Neurosurgical Associates, and Dr. John B. McCraw were the first in the country to develop a technique that reduces infection when placing the spinal column back into the body to treat Spina Bifida. This surgery was first performed at Norfolk General in 1975. (Spina Bifida is the protrusion of the spinal membranes due to a fissure in the lower part of the spine).

Charles Horton, MD, and David Allen Gilbert, MD, both of Plastic Surgery Specialists, Inc., and Patrick C. Devine, MD, and Charles Devine, Jr., MD, both of Devine-Fiveash Associates, Ltd., were the first surgeons to complete a male organ which would not require the use of an inflatable prosthesis. This surgery was first performed at Norfolk General in 1983.

Julia K. Terzia, MD, and Drs. Horton, Devine, and Gilbert were the first in the country to create a penis with erotic sensibility. They performed this successful surgery at Norfolk General in 1982.

William P. Magee, MD, DDS, J. Craig Merrell, MD, and Dr. John B. McCraw, all of Plastic Surgery Specialists Inc., removed a thirty-six pound tumor from a woman's face at Norfolk General in 1985. This was the first time a tumor of that size had been successfully removed.

The first in vitro fertilization clinic in the United States opened at Norfolk General Hospital on March 1, 1980, under the guidance of Drs. Howard and Georgeanna Jones, a husband-wife team of fertility specialists. On December 28, 1981, the nation's first baby conceived through in vitro fertilization, was born at Norfolk General Hospital. The new "test-tube" baby, a five pound girl, named Elizabeth Jordan Carr, was the first child of Judith Carr and Roger Carr of Westminster, Massachusetts. The Caesarean section was performed by Dr. Mason Andrews, a member of the in vitro team. In vitro fertilization involves the removal of a mature egg from the woman's ovary, fertilization with her husband's sperm in a laboratory dish and transfer of the embryo to the uterus for development as in a normal pregnancy.

Norfolk General Hospital, one of the nation's most innovative medical centers, has an impressive record of medical firsts. Courtesy of Norfolk General Hospital's Marketing Services Department

David Allan Gilbert,
MD. Courtesy of Plastic
Surgery Specialists Inc.

Charles E. Horton, MD.
Courtesy of Plastic
Surgery Specialists Inc.

William P. Magee,
MD, DDS. Courtesy
of Plastic Surgery
Specialists Inc.

John B. McCraw, MD,
FACS. Courtesy of
Plastic Surgery
Specialists Inc.

MILITARY

James Fort, at James-town Festival Park, is a full-scale reconstruction of the triangular palisade built by the settlers who arrived here from London in 1607 to establish the first permanent English settlement in the New World. The fort enclosed an acre of ground upon which were built wattle and daub, thatch and timber houses, a store-house and a church. Courtesy of the Virginia Division of Tourism

FIRST FORT

On May 14, 1607, the day after the first British settlers went ashore on the James River and decided to make Jamestown their permanent settlement in the New World, they began building America's first fort.

The fort, aptly named James Fort, was a half moon-shaped structure built of wood and dirt. While its exact location is not known, most historians believe that it was located about two hundred feet inward from the banks of the James River.

The first day on the site was described by colonist George Percy: "The fourteenth day we landed all our men which were set to work about the fortification." Colonists Thomas Studley and Anas Todkill stated, "Now falleth every man to work, the councell contrived the fort, the rest cut down trees to make places to pitch their tents." Studley and Todkill explained that the fortification was made "of trees cast together in the forme of a half moon by the extraordinary paines and dilligence of Captain Kendall."

The colonists quickly concluded that this half moon fort would not fill their needs in the area of protection. They were visited several times by curious Indians, but they were also attacked by hostile natives. Two settlers were killed and twelve were wounded during their first encounters with attacking Indians.

For added protection, the Jamestown colonists built a second fortification, a triangular fort, near the site of the half moon fort. The new fort was completed on June 15, 1607.

Upon completion of the second fort, George Percy wrote that the forts, with "four or five pieces of artillery mounted in them: we have made ourselves sufficiently strong from these savages."

Later the Jamestown settlers were to build at least four
additional forts to protect themselves against Indian intruders.

FIRST MILITARY OUTPOST

In 1609, after the Jamestown colonists had built fortifications for
defense against Indian attacks, they built another fort at Old Point
Comfort to ward off possible attacks by the Spaniards.

The new fort, the first military outpost in America, was called
Algernourne Fort in honor of Lord Algernon (Algernourne) Percie, one
of the directors of the Virginia Company, which sponsored the
Jamestown settlement.

The fort, built by Capt. John Ratcliffe, was a simple stockade
without stone and brick, manned by fifty men and seven cannons.

The Algernourne Fort suffered a fire in 1612, but was rebuilt. It
was discontinued in 1667.

In 1727, a new fortification was erected and called Fort George,
but it was destroyed by a hurricane in 1749.

Today on the site of America's first military outpost stands Fort
Monroe, which was begun in March 1819. It was named after Pres.
James Monroe.

FIRST CONFEDERATE SOLDIER KILLED
IN THE CIVIL WAR

The first Confederate soldier killed in the Civil War was Lt. John
Quincy Marr, who was killed June 1, 1861, in a skirmish with a small
band of Union troops near Fairfax Court House.

Marr, a lawyer from Warrenton, had formed a company of
infantry, the "Warrenton Rifles," when Virginia ceded from the
Union. The company was later designated Company K of the 17th
Virginia Regiment of Infantry.

On June 1, Lt. Charles H. Tomkins, Company B, 2nd U.S.
Cavalry, rode out from their encampment near Washington, D. C., to
reconnoiter the area around Fairfax Court House. As the Union
cavalrymen galloped through the town in the early hours of the
morning, they fired indiscriminately at buildings and persons. When
they returned later in the day, they were engaged briefly by
Confederate troops, who suffered three casualties; one killed and
two wounded.

Lt. Marr met his death by a single bullet about three hundred yards from the Fairfax Court House.

Had he lived, Marr would have been commissioned a lieutenant colonel. His letter of commission had been signed by Gov. John Letcher, but had not been delivered to him.

FIRST LAND BATTLE OF THE CIVIL WAR

The first land battle of the Civil War occurred at Philippi (now in West Virginia) on June 3, 1861, when a detachment of Federal troops from Gen. George B. McClellan's army surprised and routed a force of newly recruited Confederates.

During the last week in May 1861, a Union force under the command of General McClellan moved across the Ohio River into Virginia. Counties in the western part of Virginia had elected to secede from Virginia and had asked for federal troops to assist them in repelling any punitive action by Confederate troops.

Confederate Gen. Robert S. Garnett was dispatched from Richmond to guard the mountainous western approaches of Virginia. Garnett established a base at Beverly, and sent Col. George A. Porterfield with an advance guard to Philippi.

During the night of June 3, 1861, when Porterfield's new and untried troops were bedded down, a Union detachment led by Col. B. F. Kelley, surprised the Confederates, causing them to retreat posthaste. Because cannon fire scared away the Confederates' horses, their retreat was referred to as "the Philippi races."

Although the Philippi battle was not interpreted as a major engagement by historians, the ability of McClellan's forces to defeat the Confederates in western Virginia paved the way for West Virginia's entrance into the Union.

FIRST WOMAN TO BE COMMISSIONED AS AN ARMY OFFICER

Sally Louisa Tomkins, a nurse in Richmond, was the first woman in America to be commissioned as a military officer. On September 9, 1861, she was appointed captain in the Army of the Confederate States by a special order of President Jefferson Davis.

When wounded soldiers began arriving in Richmond after the first battle of Manassas, July 21, 1861, Miss Tomkins, originally from

Mathews County, organized a hospital in the mansion of Judge John Robertson on the corner of Third and Main in Richmond. The large house was empty, since the judge had sent his family to the country. Miss Tomkins, her four female slaves and a number of volunteers, turned the home into a twenty-five bed hospital. The first patients were received August 1.

Sally Tomkins and her volunteers worked heroically for long hours and under extreme difficult circumstances. It was their good fortune that Dr. A. Y. P. Garnett, a successful physician in Washington, D. C., cast his lot with the Confederacy and became the chief surgeon in the Robertson Hospital.

When casualties began rising, the Confederate government ordered all private hospitals closed to military patients; soldiers were to be cared for in military hospitals only.

Miss Tomkins and her supporters protested the decision to turn military patients away from private hospitals. When President Davis learned of her gallant and successful record of healing men and returning them to the ranks, he agreed to make her a captain in the Confederate Army and thus save her hospital.

Sally Tomkins' commission as captain was signed September 9, 1861, by Leroy P. Walker, the Confederacy's Secretary of War. She was assigned to the cavalry, because that branch was entitled to higher pay than the others, but Capt. Tomkins declined to accept any pay while she served in the Army.

The Robertson Hospital closed on June 13, 1865, after Richmond was occupied by Union forces. The register of the hospital showed that Capt. Sally Tomkins and her staff had cared for 1,333 soldiers during the war. Only seventy-three of them died.

FIRST PLAYING OF TAPS

The plaintive bugle call "Taps" was first sounded at the Berkeley Plantation near Harrison's Landing on the James River during the night of July 3, 1862.

The familiar haunting notes of Taps, played by buglers at military funerals and at Memorial Day ceremonies, was composed by a compassionate Union general who wanted his men to end the day to the tune of a more soothing melody than the customary "extinguish lights" bugle call.

During the June 1862 Peninsular Campaign, the Confederate

forces of Gen. Robert E. Lee prevented the troops of Gen. George B. McClellan from advancing to Richmond. One of McClellan's leaders was Brig. Gen. Daniel A. Butterfield, who commanded the Third Brigade, which was severely gored, but had repulsed attacking Confederate forces during the fierce battle at Gaines's Mill on June 27. Butterfield's brigade then covered the withdrawal of McClellan's Army of the Potomac to Harrison's Landing. On July 2, Butterfield and his Third Brigade arrived at the Berkeley Plantation near Harrison's Landing where they rested and recovered from their wounds.

As the weary troops settled down for the night, the bugler sounded "extinguish lights," which Butterfield felt was too formal. He thought that "extinguish lights" was not as smooth, melodious, and musical as it should be. He felt that the final call should bring comfort and peace to tired, troubled men.

Though lacking formal musical training, Gen. Butterfield had an exceptional ear for music. To compose a new bugle call, Butterfield formed a brief melody in his head during the night, and the next morning summoned the brigade bugler, Oliver W. Norton, and whistled his melody as the surprised bugler listened.

After hearing Norton blow the call several times, Butterfield made minor changes, and Norton wrote the notes down on the back of an envelope.

That night, July 3, 1862, bugler Norton, took his accustomed position in camp, stood at attention, and poured out the plaintive strains of the Taps we now know, loud and clear.

The music was beautiful, and immediately caught the attention of buglers of neighboring units who came to Norton the next morning to copy the music. The poignant tune quickly spread throughout the Union Army.

Taps soon replaced the three volleys fired at military funerals of Union forces so the Confederates would not know a burial was taking place.

However, quickly sensing the universal appeal of the melody echoing across no-man's-land, the Confederate buglers copied Taps. One of them sounded it at the funeral of Gen. Stonewall Jackson, less than ten months after Butterfield composed it.

The new Taps was officially adopted by the United States Army in 1874, and in 1891 the Army issued a regulation for the mandatory use of Taps at military funeral ceremonies.

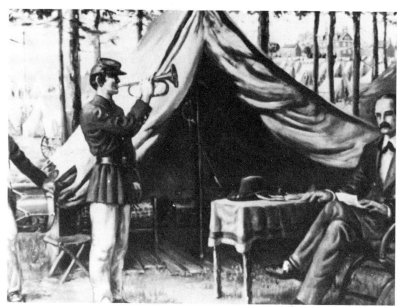

The bugle call "Taps" was first played by Oliver W. Norton on July 3, 1862 at the Berkeley Plantation near Harrison's Landing.

The haunting bugle call was composed by Union Army Lt. Gen. Daniel A. Butterfield, whose troops were then resting in the area following

fierce fighting during the Peninsular Campaign. Painting by Sidney King, courtesy of the Berkeley Plantation

The haunting notes of the bugle call "Taps" was composed by Lt. Gen. Daniel A. Butterfield during the Civil War.

These are the words the U.S. Army has adapted for the bugle

call Taps:
"Fading light, Dims the sight,
"And a star gems the sky, gleaming bright,
"From afar, drawing nigh, Falls the night."
Notes from official

U.S. Army manuals by M/Sgt. Loren R. Wilfong, The U.S. Army Band—courtesy of The United States Navy School of Music

FIRST JOINT STATE-U.S. MILITARY
ADVISORY COMMISSION

To foster closer cooperation between the U.S. military and the Commonwealth of Virginia, Gov. Gerald L. Baliles on October 22, 1986, signed an executive order creating the Virginia Military Advisory Commission.

The Commission, the first of its kind in the nation, will identify and review issues of mutual concern to Virginia and the military, and develop and maintain a working relationship between top military and state officials to address these concerns.

During ceremonies at the Executive Mansion in Richmond, the secretaries of the armed services signed an agreement to support and work with the Commission. They were: Secretary of the Army John O. Marsh, Jr., Secretary of the Navy John F. Lehman, Jr., and Secretary of the Air Force Edward C. Aldridge, Jr.

The Commission, made up of representatives appointed by the governor and commanders of various military and naval installations in Virginia, will meet at least twice a year. The first meeting was held immediately following signing ceremonies at the Executive Mansion.

Topics to be studied by the Commission include jurisdiction of state and federal agencies, educational programs and problems, transportation problems and needs, alcohol beverage law enforcement, alcohol and drug abuse, social service needs, and possible expansion and growth of military facilities in Virginia.

The military presence is important to the Commonwealth of Virginia. Federal military installations directly impact the state economy, employment, transportation system, and schools. Statewide, the defense industry puts more than $7 billion into Virginia's economy, and provides, directly and indirectly, some 200,000 jobs for Virginians.

Signatories to an agreement creating the nation's first joint State-U.S. military advisory group, the Virginia Military Advisory Commission, pose for a photo- graph at the Executive Mansion in Richmond on October 22, 1986. They are, from left to right, Secretary of the Navy John F. Lehman, Jr., Secretary of the Army John O. Marsh, Jr., Gov. Gerald L. Baliles, and Secretary of the Air Force Edward C. Aldridge, Jr. Cour- tesy of the Office of the Governor, Richmond

MONUMENT

FIRST NATIONAL MONUMENT TO THE "UNKNOWN SOLDIER"

The first national monument honoring a fallen unknown American fighting man, the Tomb of the Unknown Soldier, is located at Arlington National Cemetery, one of the United States' most magnificent national shrines and the largest of our national cemeteries. Its 612 acres are located on the gentle rolling Virginia hills overlooking the nation's Capital across the Potomac River.

On March 4, 1921, the U.S. Congress approved a resolution providing for the burial in Arlington National Cemetery of an unknown and unidentified American soldier of World War I.

On Monday morning, October 24, 1921, at the Hotel de Ville in Chalons sur Marne, France, Sgt. Edward F. Younger, U.S. Army, stood at attention and faced four flag draped caskets. Each casket bore the remains of an unknown American soldier exhumed from the American military cemeteries at Aisne-Marne, Meuse-Argonne, Somme, and St. Mihiel, scenes of heavy fighting during the First World War.

Sgt. Younger's duty was to select from these unknown and unidentified bodies the one soldier to represent all the unknown American dead of World War I for burial at the Arlington National Cemetery.

While a French military band played an appropriate air, Sgt. Younger silently advanced to the caskets, circled them three times and placed a spray of white roses on the third casket from the left. He then faced the casket, stood at attention, and saluted. A nameless American soldier, who gave his life in battle on foreign soil, had been selected for burial with honors in his native land.

The body of the Unknown Soldier was then taken by train to Le Havre, where it was transferred to the cruiser, USS *Olympia*, flagship of Adm. George Dewey at the battle of Manila Bay. The casket was placed on the flower decked stern of the cruiser for the long journey to the United States.

On November 9, 1921, the *Olympia* reached the Navy Yard in Washington, D. C., where the flag-draped casket was placed at the rotunda of the Capitol. Here the body lay in state under honor guard composed of selected men from the Army, Navy, and Marine Corps.

On the morning of November 11, 1921, Armistice Day, the casket was removed from the rotunda of the Capitol and escorted to the Memorial Amphitheater in Arlington National Cemetery under a military escort.

Upon arrival at the Amphitheater the casket was borne through the south entrance to the apse where it was reverently placed upon the catafalque. During the processional, the vast audience both within and without the Amphitheater stood uncovered. A simple but impressive funeral ceremony was conducted which included an address by President Warren G. Harding who conferred upon the Unknown Soldier the Medal of Honor and the Distinguished Service Cross. The service closed with three salvoes of artillery, the sounding of Taps and a twenty-one-gun salute.

A stately sarcophagus of pure white marble, the Tomb of the Unknown Soldier was completed and uncovered for public view on April 9, 1932. It bears the inscription:

HERE RESTS IN
HONORED GLORY
AN AMERICAN
SOLDIER
KNOWN BUT TO GOD

Since he died in the First World War, "a war fought to end all wars," the Unknown Soldier has been joined by three other fallen comrades. To the left of the Tomb, a white marble slab marked 1950-1953 indicates the resting place of an Unknown American Serviceman of the Korean War. To the right, a similar marble slab with the numerals 1941-1945 lies over the grave of an Unknown of World War II. The Unknowns of World II and the Korean War were interred on Memorial Day, May 30, 1958. An Unknown American

Serviceman of the Vietnam War was interred at the Tomb of the Unknown Soldier on Memorial Day, May 28, 1984. His grave, which rests between the graves of the Unknown Soldiers of World War II and the Korean War, is marked with a white marble slab with the numerals 1958-1975.

Honor guards patrol the Tomb of the Unknown Soldier twenty-four hours a day in Arlington National Cemetery. Buried here are the remains of unidentified American servicemen from World War I and II, the Korean War, and the Vietnam War. Also at Arlington National Cemetery are the graves of more than forty thousand servicemen and women and presidents William Howard Taft and John F. Kennedy. Courtesy of the Virginia Division of Tourism

This scene shows the burial ceremony of the Unknown Soldier of World War I at the Arlington National Cemetery on Armistice Day, November 11, 1921. The Tomb of the Unknown Soldier is the first national monument honoring a fallen unknown American fighting man. The Unknown Soldier of World War I was later to be joined by fallen comrades of World War II, the Korean War, and the Vietnam War. Courtesy of the Arlington National Cemetery

Two unknown American servicemen, killed in World War I and the Korean War, were buried at the Tomb of the Unknown Soldier at the Arlington National Cemetery on Memorial Day, May 30, 1958. Shown here is the funeral service attended by President Dwight D. Eisenhower. Courtesy of the Arlington National Cemetery

NAVAL

An artist's drawing depicts the first dry-docking in America when the seventy-four-gun ship of the line *Delaware, docked in Dry Dock No. 1 at the Gosport Navy Yard, Portsmouth, on June 17, 1833. Courtesy of U.S. Navy*

FIRST SHIP TO ENTER A DRY DOCK IN AMERICA

The first dry-docking in America occurred when the seventy–four-gun ship of the line *Delaware*, docked in Dry Dock Number One at the Gosport Navy Yard, Portsmouth, on June 17, 1833. The Gosport Yard is now the Norfolk Naval Shipyard.

An Act passed by Congress on March 3, 1827, authorized the president to order the construction of two dry docks, the first such docks to be built in the United States. The dry docks would be built at the Charlestown (Boston) Navy Yard and the Gosport Navy Yard.

Col. Loami Baldwin, one of the first American civil engineers and designer of the docks, was placed in charge of their construction.

The Charlestown dry dock was commenced in June 1827 and finished September 8, 1833, at the cost of $677,089.98. The Gosport Dry Dock was begun in November 1827, and completed March 15, 1834, at the cost of $974,365.65. Gosport Dry Dock No. 1, built of granite, is still in use today, only the caisson having been replaced as required.

Before either dry docks were completed, both shipyards competed as to which would be the first to have a ship dock in their dry dock. The Gosport Yard won when the *Delaware* entered the new dry dock on June 17, 1833. The frigate *Constitution* entered the Charlestown dry dock on June 24, 1833.

Capt. Lewis Warrington, Commandant of the Gosport Navy Yard, decided that the *Delaware* should be the first ship to enter Dry Dock No. 1, and set in motion plans for an elaborate celebration of the event.

The USS *Delaware*, displacing 2,633 tons, with seventy-four guns, was the first ship of the line to be built by the Gosport Yard. Her keel was laid in August 1817, and she was launched October 21, 1820.

To celebrate the first dry-docking, ships in the Gosport Navy Yard were decorated with flags, and galleries were erected for the invited spectators. A spacious apartment in the Engine House was set aside for the invited ladies.

On the appointed day, June 17, the shipyard gates were opened at eight o'clock in the morning so that visitors could watch the scheduled ten o'clock dry-docking. Thousands of visitors, including local dignitaries and high ranking officials from the Navy Department, showed up for the event, but they missed seeing the *Delaware* enter the dry dock, for high tide had been earlier than calculated.

What the visitors saw was the great ship resting high and dry on the blocks, and workmen beginning the repairing and recoppering of the *Delaware's* bottom. The first dry-docking in America was an unqualified success.

While the visitors may have been disappointed in not seeing the actual dry-docking of the *Delaware*, they were certain to have been pleased with the refreshments served by the congenial Commandant Warrington.

FIRST BALLOON ASCENSION FROM A SHIP

Many military "firsts" took place during the American Civil War, and one of the more unusual firsts was the use of a ship as the base for a tethered observation balloon.

John La Mountain, the first official aeronaut (balloonist) in the Union Army, had convinced Maj. Gen. Benjamin F. Butler, headquartered at Fort Monroe, that he could make aerial observations of local Confederate positions from a balloon. In July 1861, La Mountain made several balloon ascensions at Fort Monroe to observe Confederate positions on the lower peninsula.

On August 3, 1861, John La Mountain took his inflated balloon aboard the U.S. Navy gunboat *Fanny*, which then took up position in the middle of the Hampton Roads channel off Sewells Point. La Mountain ascended two thousand feet into the air in the balloon secured to the stern of the gunboat by mooring ropes and a windless. From his high perch, La Mountain made observations of Confederate forces at Sewells Point, Craney Island, and Norfolk.

This was the first time that a ship had been used as a platform to send a balloon aloft for military observation purposes.

A few days later, on August 10, La Mountain made another balloon ascension from the deck of the tug *Adriatic*.

Some romanticists like to refer to the gunboat *Fanny* as the first aircraft carrier. Not so. A balloon is not an aircraft. The appearance of the first American aircraft carrier would take place sixty-one years later.

FIRST IRONCLAD WARSHIP

America's first ironclad warship, the Confederate States Ship Virginia, *is shown in the No. 1 dry dock at the Gosport Navy Yard. Commissioned a Confederate naval vessel on February 17, 1862, the* Virginia *had been converted into an ironclad from the steam frigate USS* Merrimac. *Note the battering ram installed in the bow. Courtesy of the Hampton Roads Naval Museum*

On February 17, 1862, the Confederate Navy commissioned America's first ironclad, the CSS *Virginia*, in Gosport Navy Yard (now Norfolk Naval Shipyard).

The ironclad *Virginia* was not a new ship, but a conversion from the wooden steam frigate USS *Merrimac*, which had been sunk and burned to the waterline when the yard was destroyed by Federal troops April 20, 1861, to prevent its usefulness to Confederate forces.

The Confederate Navy was in dire need of ships to break the blockade imposed upon Hampton Roads by the Union Navy. Stephen

180

R. Mallory, secretary of the Confederate Navy, aware that ironclad ships had been built by the French and British in the 1850s, urged his naval officers to design and build a successful ironclad.

From the Gosport Navy Yard came the solution. John L. Porter of Portsmouth, a former naval contractor for the U.S. Navy, and Lt. John M. Brooke, also formerly with the U.S. Navy, each presented Secretary Mallory with models and drawings for an ironclad warship. Mallory accepted Brooke's model for construction since it was to be a seagoing ironclad rather than a harbor defense craft as was Porter's model.

On July 11, 1861, Secretary Mallory ordered Porter, Brooke, and William P. Williamson, chief engineer, to begin transforming the sunken frigate *Merrimac* into an ironclad. The *Merrimac*, of 3,200 tons, was completed for the U.S. Navy on February 25, 1856, at the Boston Navy Yard. She was one of the first six steam frigates with screw propellers built by the U.S. Navy.

The *Merrimac* was raised, her hull found sound, and she was put into drydock. Porter was in charge of construction, Brooke supervised the preparation of armor and armament, and Williamson overhauled the machinery.

In transforming the *Merrimac* into the ironclad *Virginia*, the Confederates built a barn-like casemate over her deck. The sloping sides of the casemate were timber, twenty-two inches thick, covered with four inches of rolled iron bars. Iron plates were also fastened to her deck and to her sides, extending almost three and one-half feet below the waterline. Bolted to her prow was a 1,500 pound cast iron ram.

The battery installed in the *Virginia's* pierced casemate consisted of eight guns—two seven-inch rifle pivots, two six–inch rifle pivots, and six nine-inch Dahlgren guns in broadside. Two twelve-pound howitzers were installed on deck.

The new ironclad was taken out of the drydock on February 17, 1862, and was immediately christened and commissioned as the CSS *Virginia*. Capt. Franklin Buchanan had been named by Secretary Mallory to be her commanding officer.

On February 25, 1862, the Union Navy commissioned its own ironclad, the USS *Monitor*, built at the Continental Iron Works, Greenpoint, Long Island, New York, by the Swedish inventor John Ericsson.

The 987-ton ironclad *Monitor* resembled a large wooden raft, pointed at both ends and measuring 172 feet, with a beam of forty-one feet, six inches. In the middle of her deck stood a two hundred ton revolving turret. The turret's battery consisted of two eleven-inch Dahlgren guns. The entire vessel was covered with eight inches of iron plate, including a five-foot belt protecting the hull. With only eighteen inches of freeboard, the *Monitor's* deck was awash most of the time.

Soon the two ironclads would meet in a historic battle in Hampton Roads.

FIRST BATTLE BETWEEN IRONCLAD WARSHIPS

The first battle between ironclad warships took place in Hampton Roads on Sunday, March 9, 1862, when the Confederate Navy's *Virginia* fought a four-hour duel with the U.S. Navy's *Monitor.*

The *Virginia*, which had been converted at the Gosport Navy Yard from the Union steam frigate *Merrimac* into an ironclad, had left the yard on March 8 on what was supposedly a trial run down the Elizabeth River, but her skipper, Capt. Franklin Buchanan, decided to surprise everyone by attacking the Union naval forces stationed off Newport News.

Accompanied by smaller Confederate ships and in tow by the gunboat *Beaufort*, the *Virginia* moved slowly down the Elizabeth River and into Hampton Roads. Set free from her tow about 1:00 p.m., the *Virginia* entered the James River and headed for the two nearest Union ships, the fifty-gun frigate *Congress* and the twenty-four gun sloop *Cumberland.*

Thirty minutes later the *Virginia* exchanged broadsides with the *Congress* as she passed starboard beam of the Union ship. Ignoring the *Congress* fire, which bounced harmless off her side, the *Virginia* headed directly for the *Cumberland*, which was anchored about eight hundred yards from shore.

The *Cumberland* opened fire as soon as her guns could be brought to bear, and the *Virginia* replied in kind as the *Cumberland's* shots bounded off the ironclad's armor. The *Virginia* raked the sloop with deadly fire, causing an explosion and killing many sailors.

Fifteen minutes into the battle, the *Virginia's* pointed bow rammed the *Cumberland's* starboard side, crushing her hull directly below the deck. The *Cumberland* began settling by the bow as the ironclad pulled away with her ram broken. Minutes later the *Cumberland* sank.

The *Virginia* then turned to attack the *Congress*, which had slipped her cable to get clear, but had run aground near Newport News. With her stern exposed seaward, the *Congress* had only two guns that could bear on the approaching *Virginia*. Standing within a hundred yards of the helpless frigate, the *Virginia* opened a devastating cannonade. Within minutes more than a hundred of the *Congress's* crew were killed or wounded, and the vessel was on fire. Late at night, the fire reached the magazine and the *Congress* blew up.

During the battle with the *Congress*, Capt. Buchanan was wounded in the thigh by a rifle ball from the shore. The wounded Buchanan turned over command to Lt. Catesby ap Roger Jones. As the night drew near, the *Virginia* ceased firing and withdrew to safe anchorage near Craney Island.

Meanwhile, the Union's ironclad *Monitor*, under the command of Lt. John L. Worden, had been towed from New York and entered Hampton Roads late in the evening of March 8.

On the fatal day, March 9, the *Virginia* left Craney Island about 6:00 a.m., in company of the Confederate ships *Patrick Henry, Jamestown*, and *Teaser*. At 8:30 a.m., as the *Virginia* neared its intended victim, the grounded steam frigate *Minnesota*, the Confederate sailors were surprised to see a strange-looking craft approaching.

After sending a volley of shots through the rigging of the *Minnesota*, the *Virginia* engaged the stranger, the Union ironclad *Monitor*. The two ships pounded each other mercilessly for the next four hours. The ironclads began firing at each other at ranges of about one mile apart, closed to less than a hundred yards during most of the fight, and at one time nearly touched each other. Neither ship caused serious damage to the other, except for dented and cracked armor.

During their fight, the *Virginia* ran aground momentarily. When she backed clear, both vessels tried to ram each other, but missed by inches.

When the *Monitor's* skipper, Lt. Worden, was temporarily blinded by fragments from an exploding shell, the *Monitor* broke off the engagement and maneuvered away from the battle to shallow waters.

Concerned over the receding tide, *Virginia's* officers decided to stop fighting and retired the vessel toward her anchorage near Sewell's Point.

Thus ended the historic battle between the nation's first ironclad vessels, the Union's *Monitor* and the Confederate's *Virginia*. While the *Monitor-Virginia* battle would be considered a draw (neither ship

had hurt the other), the *Virginia* had struck the Union Navy a heavy blow by sinking two ships. The advent of the *Monitor* and *Virginia* ironclads signalled the end to wooden warships in the U.S. Navy, and ultimately proved to be the precursor of the twentieth century battleships.

The two ironclads never duelled again or fought any other vessel.

As Union armies gained strength on the Virginia peninsula, the situation for the Confederate forces in Norfolk and Portsmouth became precarious. On March 10, a Union force entered Norfolk. Departing Confederate forces put fire to the Gosport Navy Yard and on May 11 the ironclad *Virginia* was blown up at Craney Island to prevent her capture by approaching Union naval forces.

The *Monitor* suffered an inglorious ending when, on December 31, 1862, she foundered and sank in a storm off Cape Hatteras.

The first "Battle of the Ironclad" was fought in Hampton Roads on Sunday, March 9, *1862. The USS* Moni-tor *(foreground) and the* CSS Virginia *(ex-USS* Merrimac) *fought to a* *standoff. Courtesy of the Naval History Division, Navy Department*

FIRST BATTLESHIP

The U.S. Navy's first battleship, the *Texas*, was launched June 28, 1892, at the Norfolk Navy Yard in Portsmouth. The twin screw *Texas* was the first steel ship built by the Yard.

The construction of the *Texas* was authorized by an act of Congress approved August 3, 1886, but the work was handicapped by American inexperience in warship design and lack of steel shipbuilding capacity.

While Congress had decreed that the ship must be of domestic manufacture, the Navy, after studying numerous construction

Launching of the Texas, *the U.S. Navy's first battleship, occurred at the Norfolk Navy Yard in Portsmouth on June 28, 1892. Courtesy of the Norfolk Naval Shipyard*

proposals, decided in spring 1887 that the best design was submitted by William John, an English naval architect.

As the result of delay in assembling the necessary mechanical appliances and facilities of a modern shipbuilding plant, and the time needed to hire experienced workmen, the keel of the *Texas* was not laid until June 1, 1889.

The *Texas* was commissioned August 15, 1895, with Capt. H. Glass as commanding officer. Her crew consisted of thirty officers and 362 enlisted men.

The Navy's first battleship, a double-bottomed vessel of 6,315 tons, had a length of 308 feet 10 inches, beam of 64 feet 1 inch. Her draft was 22 feet 6 inches. Her armor had a maximum thickness of twelve inches.

The main battery of the *Texas* consisted of two twelve inch and six 6 inch rifles; the secondary battery included twelve 6 pounders, six 1 pounders, and four 37 mm guns. She also carried four 14 inch torpedoes.

The engines, built by Richmond Locomotive Works in Richmond, produced 8,600 horsepower, enabling the ship to attain speeds of seventeen knots.

The *Texas* took an active part in the Cuban operations of the Spanish-American War.

Her name was changed to *San Marcos* in 1911, the same year she was stricken from the Navy list. She was used as a target and sunk by bombs during Army aircraft bombing demonstrations in the Chesapeake Bay in 1920.

Some historical sources claim that the *Maine*, the other battleship authorized by Congress in 1888, was the Navy's first battleship. The keel of the *Maine* was laid October 17, 1888, in the New York Navy Yard, Brooklyn, but she was not commissioned until September 17, 1895. Thus the *Texas* became the first battleship to join the U.S. Navy—one month earlier than the *Maine*.

FIRST CRUISER BUILT BY A FEDERAL SHIPYARD

The USS Texas, *the first battleship and first ship of steel built by the Norfolk Navy Yard.*

First authorized by an Act of Congress in 1886, she was finally completed and commis-

sioned August 15, 1895. Courtesy of the Norfolk Naval Shipyard

187

The cruiser *Raleigh*, displacing 3,183 tons, was the first cruiser to be built in a federal shipyard. She was launched March 31, 1892, at the Norfolk Navy Yard in Portsmouth.

Authorized by an Act of Congress in 1888, the keel of the *Raleigh* was laid December 19, 1889. She was commissioned April 17, 1894.

Capt. M. Miller served as the *Raleigh's* first commanding officer. She had a crew of twenty officers and 292 enlisted men.

Length of the *Raleigh* was 305 feet 10 inches; beam 42 feet.

Her main armament consisted of one 6-inch and ten 5-inch guns.

The cruiser's engines were built by the New York Navy Yard.

During the Spanish-American War, the *Raleigh* participated in the Battle of Manila under the overall command of Adm. George Dewey.

The Navy sold the *Raleigh* in 1921.

FIRST INTERNATIONAL NAVAL RENDEZVOUS

A travel poster depicts the International Columbian Naval Rendezvous held in Hampton Roads in April 1893. Courtesy of the Hampton Roads Naval Museum

188

The first international gathering of friendly naval powers in American waters took place during April 17-22, 1893, when approximately thirty American and foreign naval vessels assembled in Hampton Roads for the International Columbian Naval Rendezvous. The ships were gathering for the celebration of the 400th anniversary of the discovery of America by Christopher Columbus in 1492. The meeting of international naval ships had been arranged by the Hampton Roads Naval Rendezvous Association.

The festive week, which attracted thousands of spectators, featured a naval parade and drills conducted by the various ships. There were rowing regattas, bicycle races, military and trades parades, competition drills, fireworks, a grand ball, and other festivities.

The contingent of U.S. naval ships was commanded by Rear Adm. Bancroft Gherardi, commander of the Atlantic Squadron. His flagship was the cruiser *Philadelphia.*

Among the U.S. Navy ships gathered in Hampton Roads were the cruisers *Philadelphia, Newark, Atlanta, San Francisco, Bancroft, Bennington, Baltimore, Chicago, Yorktown, Charleston, Vesuvius, Cushing, Concord*, and the *Miantonomoh*, a twin-turreted monitor-type combatant that had been rebuilt after the Civil War. The cruisers were relatively new, the Navy's conversion from sail to steam now all but complete.

Foreign naval vessels participating in the Rendezvous came from Spain, Great Britain, Brazil, Germany, Russia, Italy, France, and Holland.

When the Rendezvous ended, the armada of naval ships steamed out of Hampton Roads in two columns, with the U.S. cruiser *Philadelphia* and the British cruiser *Blake* leading the procession. The ships set course for New York, where, on April 27, they participated in an international naval review presided over by President Grover P. Cleveland.

FIRST NAVAL FLEET TO CIRCUMNAVIGATE THE WORLD

A fleet of sixteen battleships of the U.S. Atlantic Fleet was the first naval fleet to circumnavigate the world. The sixteen white-painted battleships, named "The Great White Fleet," manned by some fifteen thousand officers and men, left Hampton Roads on December 16, 1907, and returned to Hampton Roads on February 22, 1909, having completed a successful 46,000-mile round-the-world cruise.

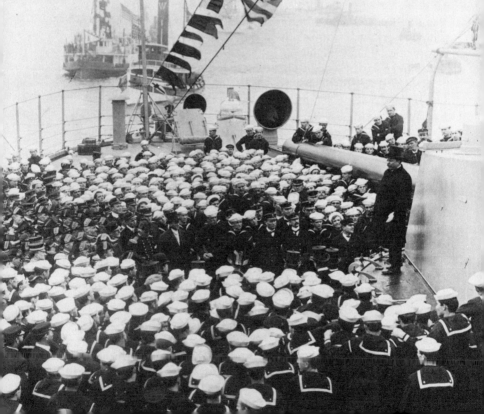

President Theodore Roosevelt welcomes sailors of the Great White Fleet home to Hampton Roads aboard the battleship USS Connecticut, February 22, 1909. Courtesy of the Hamp-Roads Naval Museum

The Great White Fleet, sixteen battleships of the U.S. Atlantic Fleet, led by the USS Connecticut, steams out of Hampton Roads on December 16, 1907 to begin their cruise around the world. The fleet returned to Hampton Roads on February 22, 1909, after having sailed forty-six thousand miles to circumnavigate the world. Courtesy of the Hampton Roads Naval Museum

President Theodore Roosevelt, who wanted the nation to have a strong navy, decided to send the fleet on the record-breaking trip to show the world the power of America's naval might. He particularly wanted to impress Japan, which was bent on expansionism in the Orient. American relations with Japan were strained during that time. Among other things, the Japanese felt that they had been cheated out of the spoils of their war with Russia in a peace treaty negotiated by Roosevelt.

Standing on the deck of the presidential yacht *Mayflower* anchored off Old Point Comfort, President Roosevelt reviewed the Great White Fleet and accepted a twenty-one gun salute from each of the ships as they passed out of Hampton Roads to sea about ten o'clock in the morning of December 16, 1907.

The fleet was commanded by Rear Adm. Robley D. Evans, aboard the flagship, the USS *Connecticut*. The fleet was organized into four divisions as follows: First Division—*Connecticut, Kansas, Vermont, Louisiana*. Second Division—*Georgia, New Jersey, Rhode Island, Virginia*. Third Division—*Minnesota, Ohio, Missouri, Maine*. Fourth Division—*Alabama, Illinois, Kearsarge, Kentucky*. Also included were a division of six destroyers and several auxiliaries.

Proceeding down the Atlantic Coast, the White Fleet rounded Cape Horn to San Francisco. Stops were made at Trinidad, Rio de Janeiro, Puntas Arenas, Valparaiso, and Calloa.

When the fleet arrived on the West Coast, illness had overtaken Rear Adm. Evans, and he was succeeded in command by Rear Adm. Charles S. Sperry. Upon the fleet's arrival in San Francisco, battleships built on the West Coast, the *Nebraska* and the *Wisconsin*, replaced the *Maine* and the *Alabama*.

From San Francisco, the White Fleet sailed to Hawaii, then to New Zealand, Australia, and the Philippines. Meanwhile, Japan had invited the American fleet to pay her a visit.

Departing from Manila, the Great White Fleet arrived at Yokohama on October 18, 1908. The Japanese went all out to be friendly to the visiting Americans, and Rear Adm. Sperry was given an audience with the Emperor and Empress between rounds of receptions and parties.

After a two-week visit to Japan, the fleet returned to Manila and then steamed for Singapore, Colombo, and then up the Red Sea toward the Suez Canal, which the fleet passed through on January 3, 1909.

After visiting several Mediterranean ports, the ships reassembled off Gibraltar on February 1, and crossed the Atlantic Ocean, arriving in Hampton Roads on February 22, 1909. A beaming Pres. Roosevelt, aboard the yacht *Mayflower*, and numerous craft saluted the returning sailors in the harbor, and an estimated sixty thousand jubilant spectators lined the shore.

The Great White Fleet was the first naval armada to successfully circumnavigate the world.

While there were those who complained that the battleship cruise had been too expensive and had left the Atlantic Coast unprotected, Roosevelt claimed that it had been an excellent training cruise for battleship personnel, and had dramatized to the nation and the world the importance of having a strong Navy.

FIRST AIRCRAFT CARRIER

The USS Langley *was converted from a collier to the U.S. Navy's first aircraft carrier at the Norfolk Naval Ship-* *yard. She was recommissioned as a carrier (CV-1) on March 20, 1922. Courtesy of U.S. Navy*

The collier *Jupiter* was converted into the U.S. Navy's first aircraft carrier, the USS *Langley*, at the Norfolk Navy Yard during 1919-1922. She was recommissioned as an aircraft carrier (CV-1) in the Yard on March 20, 1922.

The Navy's General Board decided in 1919 that the development of fleet aviation was of "paramount importance and must be undertaken immediately if the United States is to take its proper place as a naval power."

Following the lead of the British Royal Navy which was already operating aircraft carriers, the U.S. Navy selected the 12,700-ton collier *Jupiter* for conversion to an aircraft carrier. The *Jupiter*, built at the Mare Island Navy Yard during 1908-1911, was the Navy's first electrically propelled vessel.

Congress appropriated the conversion money in June 1919 and the Norfolk Navy Yard began redesigning and remodeling the coal carrier into an aircraft carrier. She was named *Langley* in honor of

Samuel Pierpont Langley, one of America's earliest pioneers in aviation.

When she was completed and recommissioned on March 20, 1922, the *Langley* had a teakwood flight deck that was 534 feet long and 64 feet wide. A hangar was built below the flight deck. An electric elevator was installed to convey aircraft from the hangar to the flight deck. Cranes were used to hoist seaplanes in and out of the water. The ship was equipped with machine shops for aircraft repair.

On October 17, 1922, Lt. Cdr. Virgil C. Griffin made the first airplane takeoff from a carrier. While the *Langley* was at anchor in the York River near Yorktown, Griffin flew a Vought VE-7SF single-seater fighter off the deck of the Langley, and later landed at the Naval Air Station in Norfolk.

On October 26, 1922, Lt. Cdr. Godfrey De Courcelles Chevalier flew an Aeromarine 39-B, a seaplane with floats removed, from the Naval Air Station, Norfolk, and made the first successful aircraft landing on the deck of the Langley as she was operating off Cape Henry.

The first pilot to be catapulted off the *Langley's* deck, on November 18, 1922, was Cdr. Kenneth Whiting, at the control of a PT-2 seaplane. The *Langley* was then anchored in the York River.

The *Langley* was nicknamed the "Covered Wagon" by naval pilots who received their flight training aboard America's first aircraft carrier.

Flying from the *Langley* was hazardous occupation at best. Planes often piled up in her crash barrier, and pilots suffered from "instrument face," caused by getting their faces bruised on the instrument panels. Luckily, there were few casualties.

After two years of experimentation, flight operations, and tests, the *Langley* left the East Coast for the West Coast to join the battle fleet. In 1937, the *Langley* was converted to a seaplane tender, and on February 27, 1942, the "Covered Wagon" was sunk by escorting destroyers near Java after being mortally attacked by Japanese bombers.

FIRST SHIP DESIGNED AND BUILT
AS AN AIRCRAFT CARRIER

The first American ship to be designed and built as an aircraft carrier from the keel up, the USS *Ranger* (CV-4), was launched at the yard of the Newport News Shipbuilding and Dry Dock Company on

Launching of the USS Ranger (CV-4) took place at the yard of the Newport News Ship- *building and Dry Dock Company on February 25, 1933. The Ranger was the first U.S. naval* *ship designed and built as an aircraft carrier. Courtesy of Naval Historical Foundation*

The USS Ranger anchored with aircraft on her flight deck. The first naval vessel designed *and built as an aircraft carrier, the Ranger took part in the invasion of North Africa in March* *1942. Courtesy of Newport News Shipbuilding*

February 25, 1933. The carrier was christened by Mrs. Lou Hoover, wife of President Herbert Hoover, who crashed a bottle of grape juice against the ship's bow. National prohibition barred the use of the traditional champagne bottle to christen ships.

The USS *Ranger*, whose keel was laid on September 26, 1931, was the U.S. Navy's fourth aircraft carrier; the first being the *Langley*, converted from a collier; the next two carriers, *Lexington* and *Saratoga*, were converted from battle-cruiser hulls. The *Ranger* was commissioned at the Norfolk Naval Operating Base on June 4, 1934.

The Ranger's displacement was 15,758 tons, her length was 769 feet, with a beam of 80 feet. Her designed speed was 29.25 knots, but she attained a speed of 30.35 knots during trial runs. Her flight deck measured 750 by 80 feet, and she had two aircraft elevators, and an aircraft hangar measuring 500 by 70 feet. Four aircraft squadrons operated from her flight deck.

Lt. Cdr. A. C. Davis made the first deck landing on the *Ranger* on June 21, 1934, flying a Vought O3U-3 observation plane.

While the *Ranger* was a welcome addition to the fleet, she proved to be too small and slow for advanced fleet aviation operations. Nevertheless, the *Ranger* contributed much to the training of naval aviators. Her aircraft were active in anti-submarine patrols in the Atlantic Ocean, and she took part in the invasion of North Africa in March 1942. After World War II she was assigned to training operations on the West Coast. The *Ranger* was withdrawn from service in October 1946.

FIRST NUCLEAR-POWERED AIRCRAFT CARRIER

The world's first nuclear-powered aircraft carrier, the 85,350-ton USS *Enterprise* (CVAN-65), was launched September 24, 1960, at Newport News by the Newport News Shipbuilding and Dry Dock Company. When she was commissioned on November 25, 1961, the 1,101-feet long *Enterprise* was not only the largest aircraft carrier built, but also the world's largest ship.

The *Enterprise* might be described as a ship which was started on a desert. A prototype ship-on-land together with nuclear propulsion equipment was built under the direction of the Atomic Energy Commission at the National Reactor Training Station in the desert near Idaho Falls, Idaho, in 1956. The desert project consisted of design, erection, and testing of a land-based prototype nuclear power plant to fulfill the requirements for the propulsion of a large naval surface vessel.

The USS Enterprise *(CVAN-65) the world's first nuclear powered aircraft carrier, is shown here in a* builder's high speed test run. The 85,350-ton carrier was launched on September 24, 1960, and commissioned on November 25, 1961. Courtesy of Newport News Shipbuilding

The world's first nuclear powered aircraft carrier, the Enterprise, *powered by eight nuclear reactors, can attain speeds in excess of thirty knots, and could circle the earth at high speeds twenty times before being required to refuel. The ship was built by the Newport News Shipbuilding and Dry Dock Company. Courtesy of U.S. Navy*

The U.S. Navy's large ship reactor program was authorized in September 1954, and on November 15, 1957, the Navy awarded the contract to build the first nuclear powered aircraft carrier to the Newport News Shipbuilding and Dry Dock Company. The keel of the *Enterprise* was laid on February 4, 1958.

A mighty ship, the *Enterprise* was equipped with eight water pressurized nuclear reactors arranged in four dual systems to drive her four propellers (each weighing 64,500 pounds). In combination, the reactors made up the world's most powerful atomic power plant, afloat or ashore. This unique plant was capable of producing more than 200,000 horsepower, driving the ship at speeds in excess of thirty knots.

In continuous operations, the *Enterprise* could circle the earth at high speed twenty times before the need to refuel arose. In 1964, the *Enterprise*, accompanied by the nuclear powered guided missile cruisers, USS *Long Beach* (CVN 9) and USS *Bainbridge* (CVN 25), made a sixty-four day around-the-world cruise called "Operation Sea Orbit."

Besides her nuclear plant, the *Enterprise* incorporates the latest in carrier design development. These include the greatest concentration of electrical and electronic equipment ever assembled on board any ship in the world. Her angled flight deck allows for the simultaneous launching and landing of planes. Her four powerful catapults, the largest ever installed in a carrier, provide an energy of sixty million foot pounds, capable of accelerating a 78,000-pound aircraft from a standstill to 160 miles per hour in 250 feet.

As a large ship, the *Enterprise* also required a large crew—4,600 officers and men, including the air groups.

The *Enterprise* was to take part with other U.S. Navy carriers in the Vietnam war.

FIRST ALLIED NAVAL HEADQUARTERS IN THE U.S.

On April 10, 1952, three years after the signing of the North Atlantic Treaty in Washington D. C., the headquarters of NATO's Allied Command Atlantic (ACLANT) was established in Norfolk.

This was the first allied naval headquarters to be established on United States soil in peace time. The headquarters site is on the Norfolk Naval Base.

The first Supreme Allied Commander Atlantic (SACLANT) was

Adm. Lynde D. McCormick, who assumed the position on April 10, 1952. McCormick served until April 1954.

The Supreme Allied Commander Atlantic (SACLANT) is by agreement a U.S. Navy admiral who is nominated to the post by the president of the United States and approved by the North Atlantic Council, NATO's highest governing body. He receives his directions from NATO's Military Committee. The Deputy Supreme Allied Commander is a British vice admiral.

SACLANT's headquarters at the Norfolk Naval Base is manned by about three hundred naval and military officers, and enlisted and civilian personnel from many of the NATO nations.

SACLANT's mission is to deter and defend against all forms of aggression within the sea of twelve million square miles, extending from the coastal waters of North America to those of Europe and Africa and from the North Pole to the Tropic of Cancer.

The maritime forces that could be made available to the Allied Command, Atlantic consists of approximately three hundred ships and eight hundred aircraft.

Flags of the nations of the North Atlantic Treaty Organization (NATO) ring the entrance to the headquarters of the Supreme Allied Commander Atlantic (SACLANT) at the Naval Base, Norfolk. Established on April 10, 1952, the SACLANT headquarters is the first allied naval command established on U.S. soil in peace time. Courtesy of Headquarters Supreme Allied Commander Atlantic

FIRST MARINE CORPS ANTI-TERRORISM BATTALION

Responding to the growing threat of terrorism, the U.S. Navy Department in early 1987 restructured its security forces to strengthen its ability to deter, detect, and defeat terrorist attacks against American interests and military personnel around the world.

As a result of revamping of naval security forces, the Marine Corps on April 16, 1987, established the Marine Corps Security Force Battalion, Atlantic (MCSF Bn Lant) at Naval Station, Norfolk.

The MC Security Force Battalion, Atlantic, was the first of two units created as part of the Navy's move to increase security forces. A sister battalion, Marine Corps Security Force Battalion, Pacific, was established at Mare Island, California, in July 1987.

The security force battalions are under the operational control of their respective Fleet Marine Force commanders.

Each battalion has a Fleet Anti-Terrorism Team (FAST) which can be deployed on short notice. The restructuring of the Marine Corps security forces resulted in Marines moving out of their traditional guard duties at naval facilities. They were being replaced by Navy personnel and civilian guards.

Unlike Marine sentries of the past, anti-terrorist MCSF Marines carry fully loaded weapons at all times.

In March 1988, a 60-man unit of the Norfolk-based first Anti-Terrorism Team was deployed to Panama to help guard U.S. interests during that country's economic and political crisis.

FIRST MAN TO BE A SERVICEMAN THRICE AND A CIVILIAN TWICE IN ONE DAY

James W. Phillips of Portsmouth registered a unique record of holding three U.S. naval ratings in one day, May 3, 1943. In so doing he became a serviceman thrice and a civilian twice in one day.

He did this by first being discharged as a private first class in the Marine Corps Reserve (the Marine Corps being part of the naval service). After being a civilian for a short time, Phillips was sworn into the Navy as an ensign, but was soon discharged. Having been a civilian again for a few moments, Phillips then enlisted in the Naval Reserve as an apprentice seaman.

This seemingly improbable record was in part the creation of the often confused military personnel policies which existed during the

James W. Phillips of Portsmouth was a serviceman thrice and a civilian twice in one day during World War II. He was first a Marine private first class, then a Navy ensign, ending up as an apprentice seaman in the Navy. Phillips is shown here wearing a midshipman uniform while holding the apprentice seaman rating in the Navy's V-12 program. Courtesy of James W. Phillips, M.D.

early days of World War II. The services created a number of enlistment programs aimed at getting young men trained and qualified as junior officers in the shortest possible time. However, the provisions and goals of these programs were often misunderstood by both recruiters and the potential officer candidates.

James Phillips wanted to become a doctor, but since his family had no financial means to send him to college and medical school, he enlisted in the Navy in hopes of saving money for an education. After a three-year hitch, he was discharged in September 1941 as a Pharmacist's Mate Second Class.

Following the Japanese attack on Pearl Harbor December 7, 1941, Phillips enlisted as a private first class in the Marine Corps Reserve officer candidate program which would enable him to spend two years in college. Under this program he first attended Elon College, later transferring to Wake Forest University. After he was accepted for enrollment in the Medical College of Virginia, Phillips learned that the Navy would commission him as an ensign and allow him to complete medical school, providing he serve three to four years on active duty after graduation. On May 3, 1943, Phillips went to the Marine barracks at the Norfolk Navy Yard in Portsmouth where he applied for and received his discharge from the Marines.

He then went to the Navy Recruiting Office in Portsmouth where he was sworn into the Navy as an ensign. While there, he learned that if he resigned his ensign commission and became an apprentice seaman in the Navy's V-12 program, the Navy would pay for all his medical education. Within hours the Navy accepted his resignation as an ensign and after a short breathing spell as a civilian, Phillips enlisted as an apprentice seaman in the Naval Reserve.

James Phillips got his medical education, and after serving the required internship and residency time, he went on active duty with the Navy as a lieutenant (junior grade) in the Medical Corps.

FIRST BLACK COMMODORE
IN THE U.S. NAVY'S SUPPLY CORPS

William E. Powell, Jr., became the first black U.S. naval officer to hold the rank of commodore in the Navy's Supply Corps when he was promoted to that rank on October 17, 1985.

Powell was born in Indianapolis, Indiana, on April 12, 1936. He enlisted in the regular Navy and was appointed by the Secretary of the Navy to the U.S. Naval Academy where he graduated and received his commission in 1959.

As a captain and commodore-selectee, Powell assumed command of the U.S. Naval Supply Center in Norfolk on May 24, 1985. He was "frocked," allowed to wear the uniform of a commodore on August 8, 1985.

Commodore was an honorary title dating back to the American revolutionary navy. Until 1862, all captains in the U.S. Navy commanding or having commanded squadrons were recognized as commodores, though never commissioned as such. Commodore became a fixed grade in 1862, then was abolished in 1899. In 1943, the rank of commodore was restored temporarily, but discontinued at the end of World War II; later it was restored as a courtesy title for Navy captains who commanded a flotilla or squadron of destroyers.

The one-star commodore insignia and rank was reinstated in 1981

Commodore William E. Powell, Jr., SC, U.S. Navy, became the first black naval officer to hold the rank of commodore in the Navy's Supply Corps when he was promoted to that rank on October 17, 1985. Official U.S. Navy photo

by the U.S. Congress to satisfy complaints from one-star Army, Air Force, and Marine Corps brigadier generals who were miffed at the Navy's policy of giving two stars to rear admirals, then the first rank of flag officers. While wearing two stars on their uniforms, Navy rear admirals were divided into two groups—the junior rear admirals lower half (Pay Grade 0-7) and senior rear admirals upper half (Pay Grade O-8). Publicly, however, a rear admiral was a rear admiral. Protocol officials often faced consternation trying to determine which rear admiral was senior to another, or who had seniority when a rear admiral and brigadier general met.

The Navy was not satisfied with the commodore flag rank; it liked all flag officers to be known as admirals. Congress agreed and passed the Defense Officer Personnel Management Act of 1986 which established a new one-star rank of "rear admiral lower half" (equivalent to a brigadier general).

With the abandonment of the commodore rank, except as an honorary title, Commodore William E. Powell, Jr., on November 8, 1985, became a rear admiral lower half, being the first black Supply Corps officer to hold that rank.

FIRST FEMALE NAVY QUARTERMASTER TO BECOME TUGMASTER

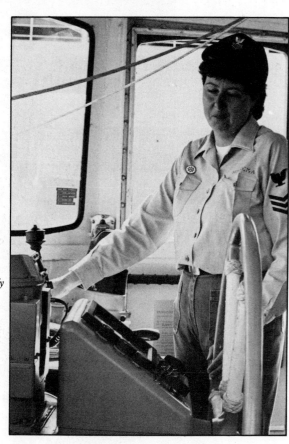

Kathleen Hoekema, Quartermaster First Class, became the U.S. Navy's first female quartermaster to qualify as tugmaster on March 17, 1986. She is shown here aboard her command, yard tug 824, at the Naval Amphibious Base, Little Creek. Courtesy of U.S. Navy

Kathleen Hoekema, Quartermaster First Class, became the U.S. Navy's first female quartermaster to qualify as tugmaster on March 17, 1986. QM1 Hoekema was stationed at the Naval Amphibious Base, Little Creek, when she earned the title of "tugmaster." Hoekema became tugmaster of yard tug 824 operating from the Naval Amphibious Base.

Throughout the Navy the designation as tugmaster carries with it the connotation of an individual possessing superior standards of professional competence, leadership capabilities, sound judgment, and personal conduct. The assignment as a tugmaster is one of the most responsible positions for which enlisted personnel can qualify.

The only ratings that can apply for tugmaster are boatswain's mates, signalmen, and quartermasters.

Earlier in her naval career, Kathleen Hoekema had the distinction of being the Navy's first female quartermaster.

FIRST FEMALE EXECUTIVE OFFICER OF A MAJOR NAVAL STATION

Commander Veronica "Ronne" Zasadni Froman became the first woman executive officer of a major U.S. naval station when she became second in command of Naval Station Norfolk on April 28, 1986. Courtesy U.S. Navy

On April 28, 1986, Cdr. Veronica "Ronne" Zasadni Froman became the first woman executive officer of a major naval station when she became second in command of the U.S. Naval Station at Norfolk.

The Naval Station, which services the U.S. Atlantic Fleet and supporting naval forces of the North Atlantic Treaty Organization (NATO), is the world's largest naval station.

As executive officer of Naval Station Norfolk, Cdr. Froman was responsible for the management of a naval organization that comprises four hundred facilities spread over four thousand acres of land. The station, which includes nearly four miles of piers, controls the movement of 1,680 naval ships annually. The station is also a major naval personnel transfer point, processing nearly thirty thousand transients annually.

Cdr. Froman entered the U.S. Navy through the Officer Candidate School (OCS) program in 1970. Since then, she has served in many challenging and varied billets and has been awarded various medals for her meritorious service.

She was hailed as one of the ten Outstanding Professional Women of the Year 1987 in Hampton Roads.

Cdr. Froman's assignment as executive officer of the Norfolk Naval Station ended in February 1988.

ORGANIZATIONS

*Mount Vernon planta-
tion, home and final resting place of President
George Washington,
became a national his-
toric shrine through the
effort of the Mount Ver-
non Ladies' Association
of the Union, the
nation's first national
historic preservation
organization. Mount
Vernon was originally
constructed in 1743 by
Lawrence Washington,
half brother of George.
Between 1754 and
1799, Gen. George
Washington developed
Mount Vernon into one
of the finest estates of
that period. The gardens
and grounds were sub-
stantially designed and
planned by Washington.
Courtesy of the Virginia
Division of Tourism*

FIRST NATIONAL HISTORIC PRESERVATION ORGANIZATION

The Mount Vernon Ladies' Association of the Union, formed to purchase and preserve as a museum the home of President George Washington, was the nation's first national historic preservation organization and the first women's patriotic society in the United States. The Association was granted its charter by the Virginia Legislature on March 17, 1856.

George Washington died December 14, 1799. His will provided that upon the death of his wife Martha, the Mount Vernon mansion and four thousand acres of surrounding land be given to his nephew Bushrod Washington, an associate justice of the Supreme Court. Bushrod Washington died in 1829, bequeathing the mansion and twelve hundred acres to his nephew John Augustine Washington, who survived him by only three years. In 1850, his widow conveyed the estate to their son, John Augustine Washington, Jr., the last Washington family owner of the estate.

The survivors of George Washington failed to take care of the property and the estate became agriculturally unproductive. In the earlier years, Mount Vernon's isolation restricted the number of visitors, but by the mid-nineteenth century roads had been improved and steamboats were plying the Potomac River, and visitors to the mansion and the tomb of George and Martha Washington increased each year. The public became uncontrollable, carrying off souvenirs, chipping away at the tomb, wandering freely and intrusively about the grounds and the house, without regard for the family. The Washingtons found their position untenable.

While the house was falling apart around him, John Augustine

Washington, Jr., tried to sell the property. His asking price was $200,000. Degrading offers came from speculators who wanted the estate for a recreation area and other purposes. Negotiations for its sale to the federal government and the Commonwealth of Virginia were unsuccessful.

Upon learning of the run-down-state of the Mount Vernon mansion from her Virginia-born mother, Miss Ann Pamela Cunningham of South Carolina, took up the challenge. Miss Cunningham, although an invalid, began an energetic drive to enlist women of America to the cause of preserving the home of President Washington as a national shrine.

Miss Cunningham's first appeal for funds to purchase Mount Vernon was made in a letter published by the *Charleston Mercury* on December 2, 1853. The first meeting to implement her suggestion took place in Laurens, South Carolina, on February 22, 1854 (the birthday of George Washington). The second meeting took place in Richmond, Virginia, on July 12, 1854. These fund-raising meetings led to the formation of the Mount Vernon Ladies' Association.

When the Virginia Legislature chartered the Mount Vernon Ladies' Association of the Union on March 17, 1856, Miss Cunningham served as regent of the Association. Each state organization was headed by a vice regent; the first vice regent for Virginia was Mrs. Anna Cors Mowatt Ritchie.

While some people refused to support any activity run by women, the country gave strong support to the Association's drive to save Mount Vernon. Of particular aid was Massachusetts orator Edward Everett, who donated the proceeds from his popular lectures on George Washington.

John Augustine Washington, Jr., stubbornly refused to sell the mansion to the Association (he was hoping that Virginia would buy the property), but finally, on April 6, 1858, Washington signed a contract to sell Mount Vernon to the Association for $200,000, with a down payment of $18,000. The Mount Vernon property was turned over to the control of the Association on February 1, 1860. The property consisted of two hundred acres of ground, including the tomb of George Washington, the mansion, garden, grounds, and a wharf and landing on the Potomac River.

The pioneering efforts of the Mount Vernon Ladies' Association in the field of preservation set an important precedent and have served as a model for many subsequent endeavors. Under the Association's trusteeship, Mount Vernon has been restored and operated without public funds or assistance from the government. It is open to the public every day of the year. Washington's home has become the nation's most visited historic house museum.

FIRST PERMANENT ARMY YMCA

The first permanent Army YMCA was organized at Fort Monroe on November 17, 1889, by Capt. Charles Bird, U.S. Army, and H. O. Williams, State Secretary of Virginia.

The commanding officer of Fort Monroe granted the Young Men's Christian Association space in the casemates of the fort. This was the home of the YMCA until a permanent building was made possible by a gift from Miss Helen Miller Gould in 1902. The breaking of ground for the building occurred on October 29, 1902.

In April 1861, fifteen YMCAs got together shortly after the beginning of the Civil War to organize the United States Christian Commission, the forerunner of today's Armed Services YMCA of the USA. Volunteers began aiding soldiers in their encampments and on the battlefields. They served as chaplains, surgeons, and nurses and distributed medical supplies, food, and clothing. The YMCA volunteers operated horse-drawn canteens, which dispensed coffee, tea, and chocolate as well as large doses of first-aid and spiritual comfort to the soldiers on the battlefield.

Today the Armed Services YMCA of the USA is a network of some fifty operating units including twenty-five branches across the nation and overseas. The Fort Monroe Army YMCA, the first permanent military YMCA in the United States, is still in operation.

RECREATION

FIRST TRASH PILE PARK

Mount Trashmore in Virginia Beach is the nation's first overground landfill that was created especially as a municipal park. Mount Trashmore, made of compacted layers of trash and garbage mixed with dirt, is the center of a 162-acre park which was opened to the public on July 14, 1973.

Faced with one thousand tons per day trash production, Virginia Beach sought means to overcome the traditional methods of refuse disposal, such as burning and open dumping, which creates numerous health and environmental problems.

Rowland E. Dorer, Virginia State Public Health Director for Insect and Rodent Control, suggested that the city dump trash in one place, compact it, cover it with earth and build a mountain. The city of Virginia Beach, the State of Virginia, and the U.S. Health, Education and Welfare Department thought Dorer's idea would work. Funds were provided by all three and the project began in 1967.

After the site for the "mountain" was selected, the area was dug out to a depth of three feet. Then the trash was spread out over the site. It was covered with a layer of soil and then rolled over by a compactor. The compactor packed the material so tightly that a cubic foot of it weighs more than one hundred pounds. After a layer of garbage and soil was compacted, the process was repeated until the mountain rose 68 feet above the flat Virginia Beach countryside.

Mount Trashmore itself covers only eighteen acres of land. It contains 870,000 tons of solid waste, and approximately the same amount of earth. At eight hundred feet long, one hundred feet wide and sixty-eight feet tall, it is the biggest hill and the highest elevation in the City of Virginia Beach.

Mount Trashmore Park is now an outstanding recreational facility with bicycle trails, playgrounds, skateboard bowls, picnic facilities, a soap box derby ramp, and two lakes.

Mount Trashmore in Virginia Beach is the nation's first municipal park to be built on top of a solid waste fill. Photo by Carole Arnold, courtesy of the Office of Public Information, City of Virginia Beach

RELIGION

FIRST STATE TO PROCLAIM
BY LAW FREEDOM OF RELIGION

Virginia, on January 16, 1786, became the first commonwealth or state to proclaim by law total freedom of religion. The statute is one of the great charters of American freedom.

At the outset of the American Revolution, a majority of the thirteen colonies still had established tax-supported churches. At the end of the Revolution, the states began to withdraw their support of official religion. Dissenters and supporters of tax-supported churches often fought bitter battles over the issue of freedom of religion.

As Virginia legislators worked to revise the legal code set down by the British Crown, Thomas Jefferson led the battle to enlarge democracy in Virginia. One of his goals was to abolish the special privileges of the established church, which was supported by taxation.

In December 1776, the Virginia General Assembly enacted Jefferson's bill to rescind colonial Virginia's official church, but vestries still retained the right to levy taxes for the poor.

The power of the churches was further weakened when James Madison in 1784 succeeded in having enacted a law which had the overseers of the poor rather than the vestries collect local taxes for welfare purposes.

The movement toward religious freedom faltered slightly when Patrick Henry, who became more conservative with passing years, proposed in 1784 that every taxpayer be required to pay a tax to support the Christian church of his choice.

Madison argued that churches should be independent of state aid, pointing out that government support was not necessary for Christianity to be strong.

While Henry's proposal won the support of the House of Delegates, it failed to pass in the Senate.

When the Virginia Legislature met in 1785, James Madison introduced a bill to establish a Statute for Religious Freedom. It was the same bill that was first drafted by Thomas Jefferson in 1779. When introduced in the House of Delegates in June 1779, Jefferson's bill was bitterly attacked, and action on it was postponed.

Madison, whose leadership and influence had been growing among Virginia legislators, made a powerful defense of complete religious freedom. So when the General Assembly met in 1785, it offered little opposition to the freedom of religion measure.

The bill for freedom of religion was passed by the House of Delegates by a lopsided vote of seventy-four to twenty in December 1785. On January 16, 1786, the Senate made it law.

The fundamental principles of the Virginia Statute of Religious Freedom are contained in this paragraph:

"Be it enacted by the General Assembly, That no man shall be compelled to frequent or support any religious worship, place or ministry whatsoever, nor shall be enforced, restrained, molested or burthened, in his body or goods, nor shall otherwise suffer on account of his religious opinions or belief; but that all men shall be free to profess, and by argument to maintain, their opinions in matters of religion, and that the same shall in no wise diminish, enlarge or affect their civil capacities."

FIRST PERMANENT SUNDAY SCHOOL

The first permanent and oldest continuous Sunday School in America was started in 1785 at the Grove Oak Methodist Church in Accomack County. William Elliott was the teacher.

While Sunday school classes were held in Savannah, Georgia, as early as 1737, none of the early classes were formed into permanent Sunday schools.

FIRST RELIGIOUS NONCOMMERCIAL TELEVISION STATION

WYAH-TV (Channel 27), the nation's first religious noncommercial television station, began broadcasting October 1, 1961, from a small studio in Portsmouth. It was started by Dr. Marion G.

"Pat" Robertson, founder of the Christian Broadcasting Network.

In late 1959, Pat Robertson, then living in New York, learned that station WTOV-TV in Portsmouth was up for sale. He believed that God had directed him to buy the station to broadcast religious and wholesome family programs to people in the Hampton Roads area.

Moving his family to Portsmouth with only seventy dollars in his pocket, Robertson began a determined drive to organize the Christian Broadcasting Network (CBN), which would operate the television station.

CBN filed with the Commonwealth of Virginia as a nonprofit corporation on January 11, 1960, and Robertson opened its bank account with a deposit of three dollars. Money to buy and operate the 17,400 watt TV station came from donations. The initial staff were volunteers. The run-down UHF television station, which possessed only one camera, had previously broadcast country and western programs.

When Robertson applied to the Federal Communications Commission for a license to operate the television station, he was told that his was the first application in the history of the FCC for a television station that was going to broadcast 50 percent or more of religious programs. In November 1960, the FCC granted CBN license to operate its TV station on UHF channel 27.

Robertson selected the call letters WYAH because they represented the Hebrew word for God—Yahweh.

WYAH-TV went on the air at three o'clock in the afternoon on October 1, 1961. Participating on the first broadcast, which lasted two and a half hours, were Robertson, Rev. Damon Wyatt, and the Branch Sisters, country hymn singers.

From a humble beginning, the television ministry of Pat Robertson over WYAH-TV has grown into the multi-million dollar cable Christian Broadcasting Network Center and CBN University, located in Virginia Beach.

Dr. M. G. "Pat" Robertson started WYAH-TV (Channel 27), the nation's first religious noncommercial television in Portsmouth. The station went on the air October 1, 1961. Robertson is shown here on "The 700 Club" set, flagship program of The Christian Broadcasting Network. Courtesy of The Christian Broadcasting Network, Inc.

SPORTS

FIRST MAN TO BE FINED FOR
WINNING A HORSE RACE

The first horses were brought to Jamestown in 1608. Like their English brethren, who were fond of horses, the Virginia colonists would eventually acquire stables of fine horses.

One English traveler, J. F. D. Smyth, noted that "Virginians, of all ranks and denominations, are excessively fond of horses..."

And like English horse lovers, Virginia colonists had a mania for racing, but horse racing was not for everyone, as James Bullock would sadly learn in 1673.

Horse racing in Virginia was long considered to be a sport in which only gentlemen could take part, although every class of the community were represented among the spectators. Betting on the horses was, of course, open to everyone.

In 1673, James Bullock, a tailor residing in York County, entered his mare in a race at Yorktown against a horse owned by a Mr. Matthew Slader for a wager of two thousand pounds of tobacco.

Bullock's horse won the race, but instead of collecting his winnings, the tailor was taken to court. Bullock, a laborer, was charged with breaking the law by racing his horse against a horse owned by a gentleman.

The York County court fined Bullock one hundred pounds of tobacco for "it being contrary to law for a laborer to make a race, (racing) being a sport only for gentlemen."

The court's decision clearly showed the social divisions that existed among Virginians. The unfortunate tailor, after winning the race, found he had no standing in the court of justice, because the loser happened to belong to a higher social grade. The unfortunate event also demonstrated the snobbishness of Virginia horsemen.

FIRST LONG-DISTANCE CATAMARAN RACE IN OPEN OCEAN

A new type of sailing boat, the Hobie Cat, began making its appearance off America's beaches in the early 1970s. The new off-the-beach fun boat, a catamaran, was little more than a canvas stretched between two fiberglass pontoons. The maneuverability and high speed attained by these multihulled boats made them popular among young sailors who liked to zip across the water at speeds of twenty knots or more.

Soon the catamaran sailors would be engaged in racing their speedy boats. One such race, the Worrell 1000, first held in May 1976, was the world's first long-distance catamaran race in the open ocean.

It all started with a dare in the early fall of 1974 over a couple of beers at a Virginia Beach bar. Two men would sail a sixteen-foot catamaran over a thousand mile course down the Atlantic coast from Virginia Beach to Fort Lauderdale, Florida.

The skipper of that brash challenge was A. Michael Worrell, a thirty-year-old Virginia Beach restaurateur, lifeguard, and small boat sailor.

Worrell survived that initial voyage, and two years later instituted—and sailed in—the first of what has become an annual catamaran race along the same 1000-mile course in open sea.

Worrell and his teammate, Guerry Beatson, also from Virginia Beach, beat out four other teams racing identical sixteen-foot Hobie Cats, in the first thousand-mile catamaran race in open ocean. The Worrell team covered the thousand-mile distance from Fort Lauderdale to Virginia Beach in eleven days, seventeen hours, ten minutes.

The first grueling Worrell 1000 was a non-stop catamaran race with the only requirement being that the contestants make a daily telephone call to tell the sponsors of their condition and whereabouts. In the interest of safety, there are now checkpoints at beachfronts in the five states of the race.

Sailors from all over the world now enter the exciting and rigorous open ocean Worrell 1000 catamaran race. In 1988, the race was renamed the World 1000.

FIRST PROFESSIONAL SAILING REGATTA

The Master of the Bay Pro/Am Regatta, the country's first professional sailing regatta, was held off Ocean View, Norfolk, in the waters of the lower Chesapeake Bay, during October 22-24, 1987.

W. Sledd Shelhorse of Virginia Beach, sailing a forty-one-foot sloop named *Prelude*, scored a sweep in all three races in Class A, for boats thirty-five feet or longer, to win the Master of the Bay trophy for being the best sailor of the regatta. Shelhorse received seven thousand dollars for winning his class and another seven thousand dollars for taking the overall title.

Ken Saylor from Hampton, skippering the twenty-seven foot sloop *Excess*, won the Class B title for boats less than thirty-five feet in length. He won one race, but finished second in two races. Saylor earned seven thousand dollars for winning the Class B title.

The races were held over distances of twelve, fifteen, and nineteen nautical miles. Corrected times were used to determine each boat's finish, with those times based on a formula computed by using each yacht's assigned handicap rating.

While some professional sailors participated in the Master of the Bay Regatta, winners Shelhorse and Saylor were amateurs. They retained their amateur standings by placing their winnings in a trust administered by the U.S. Yacht Racing Union.

The nation's first professional sailing regatta was sponsored by Bay Master Sailing Tournament, Inc., whose president, Joseph R. Huneycutt, Jr., began planning the event when the U.S. Yacht Racing Union modified rules in March 1987 that banned professionalism in American yacht racing.

Huneycutt had hoped to attract several hundred boats to the nation's first professional yacht race, but only twenty were at the starting line when the race began. Uncertainty about the event and a tiff with local watermen over fishing rights contributed to the reduced attendance.

STRUCTURES

The Pentagon, head-
quarters of the Depart-
ment of Defense, is the
world's largest office
building. Completed
January 15, 1943, the
Pentagon is virtually a
city in itself. Approxi-
mately twenty-three
thousand employees,
both military and civ-
ilian, contribute to the
planning and execution
of the defense of our
country. Courtesy of the
Department of the Defense/
Eddie McCrossan

FIRST PENTAGONAL-SHAPED OFFICE BUILDING

Located in Arlington, on the west bank of the Potomac River, directly across from Washington, D. C., stands the Pentagon, the nation's first pentagonal-shaped and world's largest office building. It was built in 1943 to house War (Army) Department personnel working in seventeen buildings scattered throughout Washington and nearby Virginia. Now the headquarters of the Department of Defense, the Pentagon is twice the size of the Merchandise Mart in Chicago, and has three times the floor space as the Empire State Building in New York.

The five-sided or pentagonal-shaped office building was initiated by Lt. Gen. Brehon B. Somervell, commander of Services of Supply, U.S. Army, who in 1941 had the scheme for housing the entire War Department under one roof. Almost immediately Somervell's proposal was met with strong opposition from various special interest groups, many who objected to the Arlington Farms site, which was for the most part a wasteland, swamp, and dumps.

As the threat of war began to draw closer, the need for additional space for the swelling ranks of War Department personnel became more acute. Consequently President Franklin D. Roosevelt was prompted in July 1941 to ask Congress for funds for additional room. After a heated debate, Congress approved of a supplemental appropriations bill authorizing and funding the construction of the new War Department building.

Construction began August 11, 1941. The prime construction contractors were John McShain, Inc., of Philadelphia, and Doyle & Russell and Wise Contracting Co., both of Richmond.

The first occupants moved into the building April 29, 1942, and the construction was completed January 15, 1943. Total cost of the project, including outside facilities, was $83,000,000. The building returned its investment within seven years.

The Pentagon building, constructed of reinforced concrete, covers an area of twenty-nine acres. Each of the outermost sides of the Pentagon is 921 feet long and the perimeter of the building is about 1,500 yards. The five stories of the building enclose a floor area of 6,456,360 square feet.

Approximately 23,000 employees, both military and civilian, work in the building. They climb 150 stairways or ride nineteen escalators to reach offices that occupy 3,705,793 square feet. They make over 200,000 telephone calls daily through phones connected by 100,000 miles of telephone cables. The Defense Post Office handles about 130,000 pieces of mail daily. Despite the 17½ miles of corridors, it takes only seven minutes to walk between any two points in the building.

FIRST ALUMINUM CONVENTION DOME

The first aluminum dome multi-purpose assembly hall built in the continental United States was dedicated on June 3, 1958, in Virginia Beach.

The $360,000 self-supporting Convention Dome was adapted from a design by R. Buckminster Fuller, an architect famous for his geodesic structures. A similar aluminum dome was built in 1957 in the Territory of Hawaii.

The dome was fabricated on the west coast by Kaiser Aluminum, shipped to Norfolk in sections, and erected on a masonry base at Virginia Beach in five days by the Globe Iron Construction Company of Norfolk. The geodesic structure weighs less than 40,000 pounds and is made up of 575 diamond shaped panels of aluminum. It is 145 feet in diameter and 49½ feet high. The dome was built to resist winds of approximately two hundred miles per hour. The dome auditorium was designed to host up to two thousand persons and fourteen hundred for banquets.

Under the guidance of Richard B. Kelley, convention bureau director, Virginia Beach's Convention Dome was the scene of many conventions and entertainment events. By the 1980s the Convention Dome had lost its luster as newer and larger area entertainment and convention facilities became more attractive.

The Convention Dome is now called the Virginia Beach Civic

Center. At one time it was renamed for America's first man in space, Alan B. Shepard. While its fate is uncertain, the Dome was considered an architectural wonder when the building opened.

The Virginia Beach Convention Dome, now the Virginia Beach Civic Center, was the first aluminum geodesic municipal assembly hall erected in the continental United States when it opened June 3, 1958. Courtesy of the City of Virginia Beach, Tourist Development Division

FIRST EARTH-COVERED SCHOOL

The nation's first earth-covered school, the Terraset Elementary School in Reston, first opened its doors to nearly one thousand students on February 1, 1977. Margie W. Thompson was the school's first principal.

The Terraset Elementary School was built to save energy. In 1973, when the Fairfax County School Board was planning a new school, the nation was gripped in an energy crisis created by the Arab oil embargo. Cheap fuel was no longer taken for granted.

To save on energy, the Fairfax County School Board decided to build its new school underground. This was done by cutting away the top of a hill, casting the reinforced concrete structure on-site, and then backfilling with dirt around and over the building.

The dirt protects from the extremes of heat and cold in two ways. First, it makes good insulation. And second, since it has high thermal mass, it acts like an energy reservoir, storing warmth or coldness and delaying the impact of outside temperature changes.

The Terraset school is solar-heated through a complex system of thermal storage and heat reclaim. The school's design was to produce annual energy savings of 75 percent to offset its cost.

FIRST DRY STORAGE FACILITY FOR NUCLEAR WASTE

On August 26, 1986, Virginia Power dedicated the nation's first above-ground dry cask facility for storing nuclear waste at its power plant in Surry.

The utility, which serves 3.5 million people in Virginia, West Virginia, and North Carolina, received a license from the Nuclear Regulatory Commission in July 1986 to use the dry cask system at the Surry Power Station until the federal government organizes a permanent nuclear waste disposal system for the country.

The first of five 100-ton iron casks purchased by Virginia Power was in place at the dedication of its Independent Spent Fuel Storage Installation in Surry. Each cask will be filled with twenty-one spent nuclear fuel rods, which had been stored in pools of water at the power station. The fuel rods contain pellets of uranium, the fuel that powers a nuclear reactor. The Surry nuclear waste storage facility, which is capable of holding twenty-eight casts of spent atomic fuel, began operating in late September 1986.

The casks were built in West Germany by General Nuclear Systems, Inc. They cost $800,000 to $1 million each.

Each cask, known as a Castor V-21, is sixteen feet high and eight feet in diameter. The cask wall of ductile iron is fifteen inches thick. A cask weighs 100 to 110 tons empty and 115 to 125 tons loaded. The cask stands upright on a pad of concrete three feet thick.

The casks will sit at the Surry power station storage pad until at least 1998, the year Congress has set for the federal government to take possession of commercial nuclear waste. The U.S. Department of Energy will then bury the nation's nuclear waste in permanent deep underground sites.

The first 100-ton iron cask of the nation's first above-ground dry storage facility for atomic waste is shown at its site at the Virginia Power plant in Surry. Standing beside the cask is Jack Ferguson (bearded), president of Virginia Power, and William W. Berry, president of Dominion Resources, Inc., the holding company for Virginia Power. Courtesy of Virginia Power

Ronald H. Leasburg, senior vice president for engineering and construction at Virginia Power, uses a model to explain how a dry cask is used to store atomic waste at the Virginia Power Plant in Surry. A stainless inner basket of the cask holds twenty-one rod-shaped assemblies of nuclear waste. Courtesy of Virginia Power

TRANSPORTATION

FIRST ROAD LAW

The need for improving the roads to better serve the social and economic life of the Virginia Colony was among the matters facing members of the House of Burgesses as they met at Jamestown in September 1632.

On September 4, 1632, the Burgesses passed the first highway legislation in American history, Act. No. 50 providing, in language of the day, that "Highwayes shall be layd out in such convenient places as are requisite accordinge as the Governor and Counsell or the commissioners for the monthlie corts shall appoynt, or accordinge as the parishioners of every parish shall agree."

This first legislation also required each man in the colony to work on the roads a given number of days each year, a custom dating at least from the feudal period of the Middle Ages in England, or to pay another to work in his place.

FIRST FERRY

The first ferry service in America was established in 1636 by Adam Thoroughgood, who had a skiff rowed across the Elizabeth River between what is now Norfolk and what is now Portsmouth.

It must have been well used and appreciated by the early colonists, because within a year the service had been expanded to three flat-bottomed boats.

The Commissioners of Peace for the newly formed County of Norfolk ordered every tithable person to contribute six pounds of tobacco toward support of the ferries.

Ferries became a common sight on Virginia creeks and rivers. In

1641, the Colonial Assembly of Virginia enacted legislation directing counties to establish and maintain roads and ferries. When the charges for ferries became too burdensome for the taxpayers, the Colonial Assembly eventually repealed the law, permitting county courts to let the ferries be operated by franchises.

FIRST TOLL ROAD

Road-building in America in the latter stages of the eighteenth century was marked by the development of turnpikes, or toll roads. The cost of supporting the Revolution had left the states impoverished, so toll financing provided a means of building needed highways with funds that could be raised by funds outside the state and county coffers.

The turnpike got its name from its toll gate. When first designed, the gate was a turnstile consisting of two crossed bars pointed at their outer ends and turned on a vertical bar or pole.

In 1772, the Virginia Legislature cleared the way for the first toll road in America, when it authorized Augusta County to build a highway over the mountain between Jenning's Gap and Warm Springs and to establish a toll gate.

The road, as provided by the Legislature, was to be financed with three hundred pounds advanced by the Virginia Colony and nine hundred pounds raised by a lottery. Revenue collected from travelers was to be spent for upkeep of the road and "towards building... housing for the reception of the poor sick resorting to the said springs."

FIRST COMMERCIALLY SUCCESSFUL ELECTRIC TROLLEY CARS

While electric streetcars had been tried in Cleveland, Ohio, in 1884 and by Montgomery, Alabama, in 1886, the world's first commercially successful electric trolley car system was installed in Richmond in 1888.

Richmond had begun to use horse-drawn rail cars in 1860, but as the city's population grew, this service became not only inadequate, but also too expensive for the rail operators. When electric power came into use in the late 1880s, the advent of electric motors was foreseen as a solution to the antiquated public railway system.

In March 1887, the City of Richmond granted approval to the

newly formed Richmond Union Passenger Railway Company to establish and operate a new streetcar system in the city. The company hired Frank Julian Sprague, an electrical engineer and inventor in New York, to manufacture and install the necessary electrical mechanism and facilities.

Sprague, a graduate of the U.S. Naval Academy and former associate of inventor Thomas Alva Edison, had organized his own firm, the Sprague Electric & Motor Company in New York City in 1884.

Sprague developed an electric trolley system using overhead power cables and a swivel trolley pole which connected the power to each car's two electric motors.

While test runs began in November 1887, the official inauguration of operations of the new electric trolley system in Richmond took place in the morning of February 2, 1888, with nine trolley cars carrying passengers over twelve miles of track. The cars. operated by five men, generated seven horsepower. By May 4, 1888, thirty trolley cars were operated by the Richmond Union Passenger Railway Company.

The Richmond trolley system, the world's first true electrical trolley system, became the standard for other electric streetcar systems throughout the nation and much of the world.

The last Richmond trolley cars made their final run on November 25, 1949, giving way to sleek new buses.

MISCELLANEA

FIRST THANKSGIVING

The first Thanksgiving in America took place on December 4, 1619, at the Berkeley Hundred, a plantation located on the James River, halfway between Richmond and Williamsburg.

This event took place two years before the first harvest feasting of the Pilgrims and Indians at Plymouth, Massachusetts, in 1621.

The first Virginia Thanksgiving service was conducted by Capt. John Woodlief, whose ship, the thirty-five foot long *Margaret*, had landed a group of thirty-eight English settlers on the banks of the James River. They had been sent to Virginia to establish the Berkeley Hundred plantation with a grant made by King James I to the Berkeley Company.

After a three-month voyage from Gloucestershire, England, they were no doubt thankful for arriving safely in Virginia, but Capt. Woodlief told the new settlers that a thanksgiving service was mandated by company owners. Specifically, the first of a long list of instructions to the settlers was:

"1 . . . wee ordaine that the day of our ships arrivall at the place assigned for plantacon in the land of Virginia shall be yearly and perpetually kept holy as a day of thanksgiving to Almighty God."

Proof of these instructions was found among the papers of John Smythe, one of the original Berkeley Hundred owners. The Smythe papers and other Berkeley plantation documents are preserved in a library in Gloucestershire, England. They were also printed in the Bulletin of the New York Public Library on March 1897, and in several subsequent issues.

Life was rough during those early years, but the Berkeley

plantation settlers worked hard and their settlement grew. Their Thanksgiving ceremony was repeated in 1620 and 1621, but disaster befell the plantation in 1622.

Early in the morning of Good Friday, March 22, 1622, Indian tribes simultaneously attacked English plantations all over the Virginia colony. At Berkeley, all of the settlers, now grown to seventy, including women and children, were massacred by the Indians.

The settlement never fully recovered from the Indians' attack. In 1691, Berkeley was acquired by the Harrisons, an energetic family which contributed much to the building of a new nation. The family produced many leaders, including two presidents, William Henry Harrison and Benjamin Harrison.

While the Berkeley Hundred Thanksgiving ceremony can be recognized as the first thanksgiving ceremony proclaimed in America, there were two earlier memorable thanksgiving ceremonies.

The first was in April 1607, when the three small ships, *Susan Constant, Godspeed*, and *Discovery* landed on the south side of the entrance to Chesapeake Bay. The ship's leaders went ashore at a point they called Cape Henry, erected a wooden cross, and knelt "to thank God for their safe arrival." Later this band of settlers established the first permanent English colony at Jamestown.

The second important Thanksgiving ceremony held in Virginia took place in June 1610 when the starved Jamestown settlers, unprepared for the rigors and dangers of colonization, were saved from disaster when Lord de la Warr arrived with a supply ship from England. The grateful settlers, on the verge of abandoning their colony and now inspired by new hope, held a service of thanksgiving, and pledged to continue their pioneering work.

As history forgot about the first Thanksgiving in Virginia, generations of Americans grew up believing the legend that the staid Pilgrims and Indians of New England inaugurated the traditional American Thanksgiving festival.

In 1958, Virginia State Senator John J. Wicker, Jr., of Richmond came across a reference to the Berkeley Thanksgiving observance while doing research for a speech. That year he formed the Virginia Thanksgiving Festival, which, on the first Sunday in November, presents a pageant observing the "First Official Thanksgiving" at the Berkeley Plantation.

Wicker prevailed upon President John F. Kennedy to acknowledge Virginia's claim as the site of America's first Thanksgiving. President Kennedy did so in his Thanksgiving Day Proclamation issued on November 4, 1963, eighteen days before he was assassinated in Dallas.

Capt. John Woodlief leads thirty-eight Englishmen in the first Thanksgiving ceremony proclaimed in America, December 4, 1619, at the Berkeley Hundred plantation on the James River. Painting by Sidney King, courtesy of the Berkeley Plantation

FIRST TOWN NAMED FOR GEORGE WASHINGTON

There are numerous towns and places in the United States
named after the nation's first president, but the town of Washington
in Rappahannock County was named after George Washington long
before he became a general and president.

At the age of sixteen, Washington worked as a surveyor to lay out
the vast land owned by Lord Thomas Fairfax beyond the Blue Ridge
in the Shenandoah Valley.

On July 24, 1749 (old style calendar), Washington surveyed and
platted an area at the foothills of the Blue Ridge where Fairfax was
interested in establishing a new settlement. Washington was aided in
the survey by John Lonem and Edward Corder.

Lord Fairfax was so pleased with the surveying job that he
named the town site after young George.

By legislation of the General Assembly of Virginia, the site
surveyed by Washington was officially established as a town in 1796
and incorporated in 1894.

FIRST STATE WHOSE OFFICIAL SONG
WAS WRITTEN BY A BLACK

Virginia was the first state in the Union to have its official state
song written by a black. The song, "Carry Me Back to Old Virginia,"
was designated as the official song of the Commonwealth of Virginia
when the Virginia General Assembly in Richmond approved House
Joint Resolution Number 10 in February 1940 after a campaign led by
the Lions Clubs of Virginia.

The song, whose original title was "Carry Me Back to Old
Virginny," was written in 1875 by James A. Bland, a black minstrel
show entertainer. The song was first performed in a minstrel show.

From its adoption as the official state song, "Carry Me Back to
Old Virginia" has been criticized for containing lyrics which do not
praise Virginia's historic heritage, and the beauty of its coasts,
mountains, and valleys.

"Carry Me Back to Old Virginny" was a ballad about the
drudgery of Negro life on Virginia plantations. The lyrics cry out for
"old Virginny...where the cotton and the corn and tatoes
grow...where the birds warble sweet in spring-time." The singer, an
"old darkey," recalls "where he labored so hard for old massa, day
after day in the field of yellow corn..."

While James Bland's lyrics declared that "no place on earth do I love more sincerely than old Virginny, the state where I was born," Bland was not a native Virginian. He was born in Flushing on Long Island, New York, on October 22, 1854. His father, Allan M. Bland, a free Negro from Charleston, South Carolina, was one of the country's first black college graduates.

James Bland attended public schools in Washington, D. C., and graduated from Howard University, where he studied music. He wrote hundreds of songs for minstrel shows, where he also performed. Some of his more widely known songs are "Hand Me Down My Walking Cane," "Dem Golden Slippers," "In the Evening by the Moonlight," and "The Old Homestead."

In 1881, Bland traveled to England where he had much success. While abroad, Bland gave a command performance for Queen Victoria and the Prince of Wales.

After a spectacular career as a minstrel show performer in England and Europe, Bland returned to the United States around 1900, but whatever he had earned abroad had slipped through his hands. Bland's musical career came to a standstill and he died penniless of pneumonia in Philadelphia on May 5, 1911. He was buried in a pauper's grave.

In 1946, through the effort of the Lions Clubs of Virginia, a monument as erected at his grave in Merion Cemetery near Philadelphia.

Although it is rarely sung any more, "Carry Me Back to Old Virginny" continues to cause controversy. Many blacks believe the lyrics are a demeaning reminder of slavery.

A recent move to change the state song took place in Richmond in February 1987, when Delegate Thomas M. Moncure, Jr., of Stafford, introduced a bill to amend its lyrics. The antiquated Negro dialect and romanticizing of plantation life would be replaced with modern praise for "old Virginia...cradle of liberty...hope of the future..." Lawmakers at the 1987 session of the General Assembly passed a resolution to study new lyrics for the state song. Since the 1988 General Assembly took no action on the matter, the quest for a new state song for Virginia remains unresolved.

EPILOGUE

Since history is the never ending process of recording human events, a book such as this should have no ending. So rather than finish with the traditional, "The End," I am employing the journalistic phrase, "More To Come."

W. O. F.

BIBLIOGRAPHY

The following titles do not constitute a bibliography of materials consulted in the writing of this book, but rather are intended to assist the interested reader in exploring further. For readers who wish to delve more deeply into some of the "first in Virginia" stories described herein, the books listed here should be helpful.

Burlingame, Roger. *Machines That Built America*. New York, N.Y.: Harcourt, Brace & Company, 1953.

Curtis, Robert I. Mitchell, John. Copp, Martin. *Langley Field, The Early Years 1916-1946*. Langley, Va.: Office of History, 4500th Air Base Wing, 1977.

Dabney, Virginius. *Virginia - The New Dominion*. Garden City, N.Y.: Doubleday & Company, Inc., 1971.

Davis, William C. *Duel Between the First Ironclads*. Garden City, N.Y.: Doubleday & Company, Inc., 1975.

Dowday, Clifford. *The Great Plantation*. Charles City, Va.: Berkeley Plantation, 1980.

Fishwick, Marshall W. *Jamestown, First English Colony*. New York, N.Y.: American Heritage Publishing Co., Inc., 1965.

Foss, William O. *The United States Navy in Hampton Roads*. Norfolk/Virginia Beach, Va.: The Donning Company, 1984.

Grant, Bruce. *American Forts Yesterday and Today*. New York, N.Y.: E. P. Dutton & Co., 1965.

Harris, Bill. *Virginia. Land of Many Dreams*. New York, N.Y.: Crescent Books, Crown Publishers, Inc., 1983.

Hawke, David. *U.S. Colonial History. Readings and Documents*. New York, N.Y.: The Bobbs-Merrill Company, Inc., 1966.

Hemphill, William E.; Schlegel, Marvin W.; Engelberg, Sadie E. *Cavalier Commonwealth. History and Government of Virginia*. New York, N.Y.: McGraw-Hill Book Company, Inc., 1957.

Hughes, Thomas P. *Medicine in Virginia, 1607-1609*. Williamsburg, Va.: Virginia 350th Anniversary Celebration Corporation, 1957.

Langdon, William Chauncy. *Everyday Things in American Life*. New York, N.Y.: Charles Scribner's Sons, 1941.

Lebsock, Suzanne. *A Share of Honour - Virginia Women 1600-1945*. Richmond, Va.: The Virginia Women's Cultural History Project, 1984.

Mapp, Alf J., Jr. *The Virginia Experiment*. Richmond, Va.: The Dietz Press, Inc., 1957.

Myers, Robert J. *Celebrations - The Complete Book of American Holidays*. Garden City, N.Y.: Doubleday & Company, Inc., 1972.

Rouse, Parke, Jr. *Planters and Pioneers, Life in Colonial Virginia,* New York, N.Y.: Hastings House Publishers, 1968.

The Tobacco Institute. *Virginia's Tobacco Heritage*. Washington, D.C.

Wertenbaker, Thomas J. *The Shaping of Colonial Virginia*. New York, N.Y.: Russell & Russell, 1958.

Whitelaw, Ralph T. *Virginia's Eastern Shore*. Richmond, Va.: Virginia Historical Society, 1951.

Whitney, David C. *The American Presidents*. Garden City, N.Y.: Doubleday & Company, Inc., 1985.

INDEX

J

Jackson, Thomas J., 86
James I, 16
James Fort, 160
Jamestown, 16, 17, 95, 106, 107, 116, 120, 160, 241
Jefferson, Thomas, 111, 218, 219
John McShain, Inc., 230
Jones, Catesby ap Roger, 183
Jones, Georgeanna, 155
Jones, Howard, 155
Jupiter (ship), 193

K

Kaiser Aluminum, 231
Kendall, George, 106
Kelley, B. F., 162
Kelley, Richard B., 231
Kennedy, John F., 241
Kennedy, Thomas, 91
Kidnapping, 78

L

La Mountain, John, 179, 180
Langley (ship), 47, 193, 194
Langley Field, 52, 53
Langley Research Center, 47, 56
Langley, Samuel Piermont, 46, 47, 194
Lawson, Walter R., 53
Laydon, John, 130
Lee, Robert E., 164
Lehman, John F., Jr., 167
Levingston, William, 23
Lighthouse, cast iron, 129, 130
Lighthouse, first, 128, 129
Lightship, 130
Lions Clubs of Virginia, 244, 245
Loomis, Mahlon, 64, 65
Lottery, 83, 237
Luray Caverns, 37, 38
Lynch, Charles, 79
Lynch law, 79

M

Madison, James, 111, 218, 219
Magee, William P., 154
Maine (ship), 187
Mallory, Stephen R., 181

Manley, Charles, 47
Marconi, Guglielmo, 64
Margaret (ship), 240
Marine Corps Security Battalion, Atlantic, 200
Marr, John Quincy, 161, 162
Marsh, John O., Jr., 167
Martin, Edward, 22, 23
Martin, John, 106
Mayflower (ship), 191, 192
McClellan, George B., 162, 164
McComb, John, Jr., 128
McCormick, Cyrus Hall, 17, 20
McCormick, Lynde D., 199
McCormick, Robert, 17
McCraw, John B., 154
McKinney, M. A., 52
Merrell, J. Craig, 154
Merrimac (ship), 180, 181, 182
Miller, M., 188
Minnesota (ship), 183
Mitchell, William "Billy," 52, 53
Moncure, Thomas M., Jr., 245
Monitor (ship), 181, 182, 183, 184
Monroe, James, 111, 144
Morrow, Charles, 124
Mount Trashmore, 214, 215
Mount Vernon Ladies' Association, 210, 211
Mount Vernon Mansion, 208, 209, 210, 211, 212
Music School, Navy, 91, 92

N

Naval Rendezvous, 189
Naval Station, Norfolk, 205, 206
Naval Supply Center, Norfolk, 202
New Market Battle, 87
Newport, Christopher, 94, 95, 106, 116, 142
Newport News Shipbuilding and Dry Dock Company, 194, 196, 198
Norfolk Navy Yard, 178, 185, 188, 193
Northampton County tax grievances, 109, 110
Norton, Oliver W., 164
Norton, William, 116
Nuclear waste storage, 233

ABOUT THE AUTHOR

History has long been the interest of William O. Foss, journalist and writer, whose numerous articles have appeared in national magazines. Two of his previously published books dealt with Virginia subjects—*The United States Navy in Hampton Roads* and *The Norwegian Lady and the Wreck of the Dictator*, the story of an 1891 shipwreck off the coast of Virginia Beach. He has also written books about skiing, oceanography, the Marine Corps, and the Coast Guard. Foss and his wife Dulcie make their home in Virginia Beach, Virginia.